Black Americans of Achievement

LEGACY EDITION

Frederick Douglass

Abolitionist Editor

Black Americans of Achievement

LEGACY EDITION

Black Americans of Achievement

LEGACY EDITION

Frederick Douglass

Abolitionist Editor

Sharman Apt Russell

With additional text written by
Heather Lehr Wagner

Consulting Editor, Revised Edition
Heather Lehr Wagner

Senior Consulting Editor, First Edition
Nathan Irvin Huggins
Director, W.E.B. Du Bois Institute
for Afro-American Research
Harvard University

CHELSEA HOUSE
P U B L I S H E R S
A Haights Cross Communications Company
Philadelphia

COVER: Late nineteenth-century portrait of Douglass.

CHELSEA HOUSE PUBLISHERS

VP, NEW PRODUCT DEVELOPMENT Sally Cheney
DIRECTOR OF PRODUCTION Kim Shinners
CREATIVE MANAGER Takeshi Takahashi
MANUFACTURING MANAGER Diann Grasse

Staff for FREDERICK DOUGLASS

EXECUTIVE EDITOR Lee Marcott
ASSISTANT EDITOR Alexis Browsh
PRODUCTION EDITOR Noelle Nardone
PHOTO EDITOR Sarah Bloom
SERIES AND COVER DESIGNER Keith Trego
LAYOUT 21st Century Publishing and Communications, Inc.

Library of Congress Cataloging-in-Publication Data

Russell, Sharman Apt.
   Frederick Douglass : abolitionist editor/Sharman Apt Russell; with additional text by
Heather Lehr Wagner.
      p. cm.—(Black Americans of achievement)
Includes bibliographical references and index.
   ISBN 0-7910-8157-5 — ISBN 0-7910-8331-4 (pbk.)
   1. Douglass, Frederick, 1818–1895. 2. Abolitionists—United States—Biography. 3. African
American abolitionists—Biography. 4. Slaves—United States—Biography. 5. Antislavery
movements—United States—History—19th century. I. Wagner, Heather Lehr. II. Title.
III. Series.
E449.D75R875 2004
973.8'092—dc22

2004008473

Contents

Introduction

Nearly 20 years ago Chelsea House Publishers began to publish the first volumes in the series called BLACK AMERICANS OF ACHIEVEMENT. This series eventually numbered over a hundred books and profiled outstanding African Americans from many walks of life. Today, if you ask school teachers and school librarians what comes to mind when you mention Chelsea House, many will say—"Black Americans of Achievement."

The mix of individuals whose lives we covered was eclectic, to say the least. Some were well known—Muhammad Ali and Dr. Martin Luther King, Jr, for example. But others, such as Harriet Tubman and Sojourner Truth, were lesser-known figures who were introduced to modern readers through these books. The individuals profiled were chosen for their actions, their deeds, and ultimately their influence on the lives of others and their impact on our nation as a whole. By sharing these stories of unique Americans, we hoped to illustrate how ordinary individuals can be transformed by extraordinary circumstances to become people of greatness. We also hoped that these special stories would encourage young-adult readers to make their own contribution to a better world. Judging from the many wonderful letters we have received about the BLACK AMERICANS OF ACHIEVEMENT biographies over the years from students, librarians, and teachers, they have certainly fulfilled the goal of inspiring others!

Now, some 20 years later, we are publishing 18 volumes of the original BLACK AMERICANS OF ACHIEVEMENT series in revised editions to bring the books into the twenty-first century and make them available to a new generation of young-adult readers. The selection was based on the importance of these figures to American life and the popularity of the original books with our readers. These revised editions have a new full-color design and, wherever possible, we have added color photographs. The books have new features, including quotes from the writings and speeches of leaders and interesting and unusual facts about their lives. The concluding section of each book gives new emphasis to the legacy of these men and women for the current generation of readers.

The lives of these African-American leaders are unique and remarkable. By transcending the barriers that racism placed in their paths, they are examples of the power and resiliency of the human spirit and are an inspiration to readers.

We present these wonderful books to our audience for their reading pleasure.

Lee M. Marcott
Chelsea House Publishers
August 2004

The Fortunate Meeting

In August 1841, a group of men and women gathered at the Atheneum hall on the island of Nantucket. They were members of the Massachusetts Anti-Slavery Society, and their goal was to abolish the inhumane system of slavery that existed throughout the southern United States, where millions of black people were held in bondage. The abolitionists, as those who were fighting against slavery were called, were morally opposed to the practice of buying and selling fellow human beings. They were determined that all people living in America should enjoy the rights to life, liberty, and the pursuit of happiness.

Among those attending the abolitionist meeting was Frederick Douglass, a young black man who had escaped from slavery in Maryland almost three years before. Tall, strong, with a thick mane of hair, the 23-year-old Douglass was strikingly handsome. Ever since he had gained his freedom, moved to the Massachusetts port town of New Bedford, and changed

1

his name from Bailey to Douglass to hide his identity, he had attended meetings of the American Anti-Slavery Society and subscribed to the organization's newspaper, the *Liberator*. He also preached at a local black church, mixing biblical teachings with his reflections on the evils of slavery. A man who always seemed to be working, Douglass decided in the summer of 1841 to take a brief vacation and go to the meeting on Nantucket.

As Douglass sat waiting for the speakers to appear, he was not aware that his name had come to the attention of the leaders of the abolitionist movement. Most of the people in the hall were strangers to him. Consequently, he was amazed when William Coffin, an abolitionist from New Bedford, approached him and asked if he would address the crowd. Coffin had heard Douglass speak in church and was impressed by the intelligent, self-educated ex-slave. He was sure that Douglass's stories of his years as a slave named Frederick Bailey would have a strong effect on the audience.

Although Douglass accepted Coffin's invitation, he was so nervous that he could barely stand up. Once on the speaker's platform, the normally articulate young man stammered and hesitated. His listeners called out to encourage him, and, little by little, Douglass was able to explain to them what it was like to be a slave. He told how he had been separated from his mother soon after birth. He told about the awful beatings he endured and about the times he had been overworked and passed out from exhaustion—and been beaten. He also told how he had learned to read and write, how he had become a skilled tradesman, and how he had then escaped to freedom. Finally, he told the audience how important the abolitionist movement was to former slaves.

Douglass's words impressed the New England crowd. Most of the people attending the meeting were white, and few had ever seen a slave or listened to a black person tell about his life. Deeply religious, they believed that owning slaves was

After escaping from slavery, Frederick Douglass became world-renowned for his writing and speaking skills and was one of the most important members of the American abolitionist movement.

sinful. Only a handful knew about the brutal conditions under which the majority of slaves lived. Many people in the North accepted statements made by Southern slaveowners that blacks were inferior to whites, that they were happy as slaves, and that they were good only for menial tasks and hard labor. When they listened to Frederick Douglass, a man who had been raised a slave and yet who stood before the audience proudly displaying the broad knowledge he had gained during his years of servitude, they felt even more

deeply convinced of the necessity for black emancipation—
for the freeing of all slaves.

When Douglass finished his speech, the audience gave him a
deafening round of applause, cheering him for all that he
had accomplished in the face of such injustice. The abolitionists
appreciated Douglass's courage in speaking to them, for though
he lived in a state where slavery was illegal, under federal law he
was still a fugitive slave. If his whereabouts became known, his
former owner would be within his rights to send a slave hunter
to kidnap Douglass and bring him back to Maryland in chains.

Douglass was followed on the speaker's platform by William
Lloyd Garrison, one of the leading spokesmen of the abolitionist movement. Garrison was as thrilled by Douglass's words
as everyone else in the hall. Never, he declared, had a person
given a more moving speech in support of liberty. When he
asked the abolitionists if they would ever allow Douglass to
be returned to slavery, they shouted, "No." They promised to
protect Douglass and other fugitive slaves, even if it meant
breaking the law.

IN HIS OWN WORDS...

On October 23, 1845, Frederick Douglass delivered a speech in Cork, Ireland,
denouncing American prejudice against blacks. He passionately argued
against any possible justification of slavery:

> In no sound philosophy can slavery be justified. 'Tis at war with the best
> feelings of the human heart. 'Tis at war with Christianity. Wherever we find
> an individual justify[ing] slavery on such a pretext you will find him
> also justifying the slavery of any human beings on the earth. 'Tis the old
> argument on the part of tyrants. Tyrants have ever justified their tyranny by
> arguing on the inferiority of their victims. The Slavery of only part or portion
> of the human family, is a matter of interest to every member of the human
> family; slavery being the enemy of all mankind.

At the end of the meeting, Douglass agreed to take a position as a traveling agent of the American Anti-Slavery Society. During the next three years, he would speak in towns and cities throughout the northern United States. In some places he would win converts to the cause of black emancipation; in others, he would be beaten by hostile crowds. He carried on with his task, and in 1845, with the publication of the first of his autobiographical works, *Narrative of the Life of Frederick Douglass, an American Slave,* he would become known throughout the world as a leader of the antislavery movement. As an editor, writer, and speaker, Douglass would play a major role in helping to end the ugly institution that divided his country between those who favored human freedom and those who relied on the forced labor of others.

Douglass's attendance at the Nantucket meeting was, as William Lloyd Garrison wrote in his preface to the *Narrative,* a "most fortunate occurrence. . . . Fortunate," he wrote, "for the cause of negro emancipation, and of universal liberty." Garrison was among the first to feel the powerful force of Douglass's attack on human bondage and was moved to write of that experience, "I think I never hated slavery so intensely as at that moment." Frederick Douglass would arouse this feeling in many people before his long struggle for black freedom and rights was over.

2

Freedom's Rainbow

The slave Frederick Bailey was born in February 1818 on Holmes Hill farm, near the town of Easton on Maryland's Eastern Shore. The farm was part of an estate owned by Aaron Anthony, a former ship's captain and the manager of the plantations belonging to Edward Lloyd V, one of the wealthiest men in Maryland. The main Lloyd plantation was near the eastern side of the Chesapeake Bay, 12 miles from Holmes Hill farm, and it was there, in a house he had built near the Lloyd mansion, that Frederick's first master lived.

Frederick's mother, tall, dark Harriet Bailey, worked in the cornfields surrounding Holmes Hill. It was from her that he got his last name. He knew little about his father except that the man was white—as a child he would hear rumors that the master himself, Captain Anthony, had been his father.

Because Harriet Bailey was required to work long hours in the fields, Frederick was separated from his mother soon after birth and was sent to live with his grandmother, Betsey Bailey. The mother of three sons and nine daughters, many of whom worked on Anthony's lands, Betsey Bailey lived in a cabin a short distance from Holmes Hill farm. Her job was to look after Harriet's children until they were old enough to work.

In his earliest years, Frederick did not think of himself as a slave. His mother visited him when she could, but he had only a hazy memory of her. He spent many happy days playing in the woods by his grandmother's cabin, and only gradually did he begin to learn about a mysterious person called Old Master, whose name Betsey Bailey spoke with fear.

One morning, when Frederick was about six years old, his grandmother told him that they were going on a long journey. They set off down the road leading westward, with Frederick clinging to his grandmother's skirts as they walked for mile after mile. Finally, the old woman and the boy reached a large, elegant house, around which were playing many children.

Frederick's grandmother pointed out to him his brother Perry and his sisters Sarah and Eliza among the children in the yard. The boy was confused, not understanding who these children were, but he had a feeling that something bad was about to happen. When his grandmother told him to join the others, he did so reluctantly, but he refused to play with them. After a while, one of the children ran up to Frederick and yelled at him that his grandmother was gone. He collapsed on the ground and wept. The happy years at his grandmother's cabin had ended.

Frederick later wrote, "This was my first introduction to the realities of the slave system." More painful lessons were to follow. The slave children of Captain Anthony's household were fed cornmeal mush that was placed in a trough, to which they were called, Frederick later wrote, "like so many pigs." Using oyster shells and other homemade spoons, the hungry children competed with each other for every bit of the gruel. A linen shirt that hung to their knees was all that they were given to wear. None had beds or warm blankets. They suffered miserably on cold winter nights, huddling in recesses in the kitchen of the Anthony house. "My feet have been so cracked with frost," Frederick noted later, "that the pen with which I am writing might be laid in the gashes."

One of Frederick's worst experiences was the first time he saw a whipping take place. One night he was woken by a woman's screams. Peering through a crack in the wall of the kitchen, he saw Captain Anthony lashing the bare back of Hester Bailey, Frederick's aunt, with a heavy cowskin whip. Terrified, Frederick forced himself to watch the woman's whole long ordeal. In the coming years, he was to see many slaves whipped by their masters. Occasionally, he himself would be the victim. Although some masters were relatively kind, others, like Captain Anthony, beat their slaves brutally if they did not obey orders quickly enough.

Because Frederick's mother worked 12 miles from the Lloyd plantation, she was rarely able to visit her children there. Frederick saw her for the last time when he was seven years old. He remembered her giving a severe scolding to the mean household cook who disliked Frederick and gave him little food. A few months after the visit, Harriet Bailey died, but Frederick did not learn about this until much later.

LIFE IN BALTIMORE

Overall, Frederick was luckier than most of the slave children. He had a natural charm that many people found engaging, and he was chosen to be the companion of Daniel Lloyd, the youngest son of the plantation's owner. Frederick's chief friend and protector was Lucretia Auld, Aaron Anthony's daughter, who had recently married a ship's captain named Thomas Auld. She seemed to think that Frederick was a special child.

One day in 1826, Lucretia Auld told Frederick that he was being sent to live with her brother-in-law, Hugh Auld, who managed a shipbuilding firm in Baltimore, Maryland. She told him that if he scrubbed himself clean, she would give him a pair of trousers. Frederick was overjoyed at this chance to escape the life of a field hand. He cleaned himself and won his first pair of pants. Within three days he was on his way to the busy port of Baltimore.

At first Frederick got along extremely well with his new masters. Sophia, Hugh Auld's wife, had never owned a slave before and did not know the "proper" way to treat one. She disliked the servile manners that Frederick had been taught on the plantation, and she told him to look her in the eye when he spoke to her. Frederick's only jobs were to run errands and care for and entertain the Aulds' infant son, Tommy. It was pleasant work for Frederick, and he grew to love the little boy.

A religious woman, Sophia Auld frequently read aloud from the Bible. Intrigued, Frederick asked his mistress to teach him how to read, and she readily consented. He soon mastered the alphabet and a few simple words. Proud of her pupil's progress, Sophia Auld told her husband what she had done. Hugh Auld

IN HIS OWN WORDS...

In *Narrative of the Life of Frederick Douglass,* Douglass recalled how reading transformed his life:

> The more I read, the more I was led to abhor and detest my enslavers. I could regard them in no other light than a band of successful robbers, who had left their homes, and gone to Africa, and stolen us from our homes, and in a strange land reduced us to slavery. I loathed them as being the meanest as well as the most wicked of men. . . . I would at times feel that learning to read had been a curse rather than a blessing. It had given me a view of my wretched condition, without the remedy. I opened my eyes to the horrible pit, but to no ladder upon which to get out. . . . It was this everlasting thinking of my condition that tormented me. There was no getting rid of it. It was pressed upon me by every object within sight or hearing, animate or inanimate. The silver trump of freedom had roused my soul to eternal wakefulness. Freedom now appeared, to disappear no more forever.

was furious. Teaching a slave to read was unlawful, he said. It made a slave unfit for his work—namely, obeying his master without question or thought. A slave who knew how to read and write could forge papers that said he was free and then escape to one of the states in the North, where slavery was outlawed.

Sophia Auld heeded her husband's orders and stopped the lessons. Frederick had learned a great deal from Hugh Auld's outburst. If learning how to read and write made him unfit to be a slave and was the pathway to freedom, then gaining this knowledge would be his goal. Once in command of the alphabet, he progressed quickly on his own. He made friends with poor white children he met on his errands and used them as teachers, paying for his reading lessons with pieces of bread.

At home, Frederick read parts of books and newspapers when he could, but he had to be constantly on guard against his mistress. Sophia Auld had taken the words of her husband to heart, and she screamed at Frederick whenever she saw him looking at reading material. The change in his mistress troubled Frederick, who began to see that slavery was a "fatal poison" for the owner as well as the slave. As he wrote later about Sophia Auld, "She at first regarded me as a child, like any other. . . . When she came to consider me as property, our relations to each other changed."

Still, Frederick gradually learned both how to read and write. While doing small jobs at Hugh Auld's shipyard, he watched the workmen label timbers and masts with letters to indicate where the pieces would be used. Frederick copied these letters and soon learned how to write whole words. With a little money he earned doing errands, he bought a copy of *The Columbian Orator*, a collection of speeches and essays dealing with liberty, democracy, and courage. In one of the pieces, a master and his slave discuss the institution of slavery, and they finally agree that it is wrong to hold another man in bondage.

Frederick was strongly affected by the speeches on freedom in *The Columbian Orator*, and by reading the local newspapers he began to learn about abolitionists—men and women who were fighting to end slavery in the United States. He also read about the slave rebellion led by Nat Turner in Virginia in 1831. The fiery preacher Turner organized an army of slaves that

Nat Turner

Nat Turner was born a slave in Southampton County, Virginia, in October 1800. As a child and then later as an adult, Turner spoke of dreams and visions, including vivid descriptions of events that had happened before his birth. His unique behavior and intense focus on fasting and prayer caused others to view him as special and a kind of prophet.

When he was about 20 years old, Turner ran away from his master but returned after 30 days because a vision had told him to go back to his life as a slave. Other visions soon followed, including one in which he saw figures of men outlined in the heavens and another in which he was told that a sign would appear in the heavens as a signal for him to fight against his evil enemies using their own weapons to kill them.

In February 1831, an eclipse of the sun provided the sign that had been described in Turner's vision. He outlined a plan to four fellow slaves he trusted, and a slave revolt was scheduled for July 4. An illness caused Turner to postpone the planned rebellion until another atmospheric change. This time, August 13, the change caused the sun to seem blue-green in the sky. Turner viewed this as a definitive sign that the time had come. On August 21, Turner and six men met in the woods and finalized their plans. Long after midnight, they went to the home of Turner's owners, killing the entire family as they slept. They continued, going from house to house and killing every white person they found. They were joined by other slaves, and soon the group numbered more than 60.

As Turner's "army" headed for the nearest town, Jerusalem, whites organized a militia to respond to the attacks. Turner's force met with resistance and soon fell apart. Some were captured, but others (including Turner) escaped. Turner hid for several days but was captured on October 30. While in prison, he dictated a "Confession," which outlined his experiences and beliefs. Turner was ultimately hanged and skinned for his part in the murders of over 50 white people during the revolt he organized. Turner was one of dozens of black people executed for the rebellion; angry white mobs separately murdered 200 blacks, many of whom were innocent of any role in Nat Turner's rebellion.

went on a rampage, massacring all the slaveholders in its path. Federal and state troops finally crushed the uprising, but many American slaves honored Turner as a great freedom fighter.

Not yet 13 years old but afire with new ideas that both tormented and inspired him, Frederick began to loathe slavery with a passion. "I had penetrated to the secret of all slavery and oppression," he wrote. "Slaveholders are only a band of successful robbers." His dreams of emancipation were encouraged by the example of other blacks in Baltimore, most of whom were free. Unfortunately, new laws passed by Southern state legislatures had made it increasingly difficult for owners to free their slaves.

During this time, Aaron Anthony died, and his property fell to his two sons and his daughter, Lucretia Auld. Frederick was still part of the Anthony estate, and so he was sent back to the Lloyd plantation to be part of the division of property. Lined up beside his brothers, sisters, aunts, and cousins to be ranked and valued with the horses, sheep, and pigs, Frederick prayed that he would not be chosen by the captain's eldest son, the cruel drunkard Andrew Anthony. The man had already wasted much of his inheritance, and any slave chosen by him was likely to be sold to slave traders and taken to Georgia, Alabama, or another state in the Deep South, where it would be nearly impossible for a slave to gain his freedom.

Fortunately, Frederick was selected by Thomas and Lucretia Auld and was sent back to Hugh and Sophia Auld in Baltimore. Seeing his family divided strengthened his hatred of slavery, however, and he was especially upset that his grandmother, considered to be too old for any work, was turned out of her cabin and sent into the woods to die.

Within a year of Frederick's return to Baltimore, Lucretia Auld died. The two Auld brothers then got into a dispute, and Thomas wrote to Hugh demanding the return of his late wife's property, which included Frederick. Frederick was sorry to leave Baltimore. He had recently become a teacher to a group of other young blacks. In addition, a black preacher named

For Douglass, one very disturbing part of the slave system was the dissolution of families. When a master died, his slave property was inherited by family or sold at an auction, like the one seen here, without any consideration of slave relationships.

Charles Lawson had adopted him as a spiritual son, telling the young man that he was destined to become a religious leader. Unlike these men, Frederick was a slave, and, in March 1833, the 15-year-old was forced to leave his friends behind and go to Thomas Auld's new farm near the town of St. Michaels, a few miles from the Lloyd plantation.

REBELLIOUS FIELD HAND

Frederick was extremely unhappy with his new situation as a field hand on the farm. Thomas Auld starved his slaves, and they had to steal food from neighboring farms to stay alive. The sullen Frederick received many beatings, and he saw worse ones given to an awkward slave whose hands had been crippled in a fire. He organized a Sunday religious service for the slaves in the area, but the group met in St. Michaels only a few times before it was broken up by a mob led by Thomas Auld.

Frederick had little liking for white clergymen, for they preached that it was a slave's duty to obey his master. The hypocrisy of his master, who was known as one of the most devout men in the neighborhood, appalled Frederick. Thomas Auld whipped his slaves while reading from the Bible. A bad manager, he knew little about farming, and he found Frederick especially difficult to control. At last, Auld decided to have someone tame his unruly slave for him.

In January 1834, Frederick was sent to work for Edward Covey, a poor farmer who had gained a reputation around St. Michaels for being a skilled "slave breaker." Covey seldom needed to rent field hands because richer farmers loaned him their slaves so that he could train them to be obedient workers. The only benefit that Frederick received from his transfer was that Covey fed his slaves better than Auld did.

Like the other slaves on Covey's farm, Frederick worked from dawn until after nightfall, plowing, hoeing, and picking corn. Although the men were given plenty of food, they were allowed only a few minutes to gobble it down before they were forced to return to their labor. They always had to be on the lookout for Covey because he hid behind bushes and spied on them as they worked. When the farmer caught a slave resting, he would beat him with thick branches.

After only one week on the farm, Frederick let an oxen team run wild and was given a serious beating by Covey. During the following months, he was continually whipped until he began to feel that he was indeed broken. On a hot afternoon in August, his strength finally failed him and he collapsed in the dirt. Covey kicked and beat him and then stalked off in disgust. Frederick at last managed to get up and walk to the Auld farm, where he pleaded with his master to let him stay. Auld had little sympathy for his desperate slave and sent him back to Covey.

Beaten down though he was, Frederick found the strength to rebel when Covey began tying him to a post in preparation for another whipping. "At that moment—from whence came the spirit I don't know—I resolved to fight," Frederick wrote. "I seized Covey hard by the throat, and as I did so, I rose." The two men battled for almost two hours. Covey finally gave up, telling Frederick that he would have been whipped less severely if he had not resisted. "The truth was," said Frederick, "that he had not whipped me at all."

Frederick had discovered an important truth: "Men are whipped oftenest who are whipped easiest." He was lucky; legally, a slave could be killed for resisting his master. Covey, though, had a reputation to protect and did not want it known that he could not control a 16-year-old boy. Frederick was never beaten during the rest of his time on Covey's farm.

PLOTTING ESCAPE

After a year's service with Covey, Frederick was sent to work for a farmer named William Freeland, a relatively kind master. By now, though, Frederick wanted more than kindness; he wanted his freedom. He started an illegal school for blacks in the area that met secretly at night and on Sundays, and with five other slaves he began to plot an escape to the North.

After working for a year on Freeland's farm, Frederick was ready to leave. His group planned to steal a boat, row to the northern tip of Chesapeake Bay, and then flee on foot to the free state of Pennsylvania. Just before the Easter holiday in 1836, when the escape was supposed to take place, a band of armed white men seized the slaves and threw them in jail. One of Frederick's associates had exposed the plot.

Frederick was imprisoned for about a week. While in jail, he was inspected by slave traders, and he fully expected that he would be sold to "a life of living death" in the Deep South. To his surprise, Thomas Auld came and released him. Instead of shipping his unmanageable slave to the Alabama cotton fields, Frederick's master sent him back to Hugh Auld in Baltimore. The two brothers had finally settled their dispute.

More than three years had passed since Frederick had left Baltimore. The 18 year old was now six feet tall and very strong from his days in the fields. Hugh Auld decided that Frederick should earn his keep by working as a caulker—a man who forced sealing matter into the seams in a boat's hull to make it watertight. He was hired out to a local shipbuilder so that he could learn the trade.

While apprenticing at the shipyard, Frederick was harassed by white workers who did not want blacks—no matter whether they were slaves or freemen—competing with them for jobs. One afternoon, a group of white apprentices beat up Frederick and nearly took out one of his eyes. Hugh Auld was angry when he saw what had happened to his slave, and he attempted to press charges against Frederick's assailants. None of the shipyard's white employees would step forward and testify about the beating, so the case had to be dropped. Free blacks had little hope of obtaining justice through the Southern court system, which refused to accept a black person's testimony against a white person. A slave like Frederick had no chance at all.

After Frederick recovered from his injuries, he began apprenticing at the shipyard where Hugh Auld worked. Within a year, he was an experienced caulker and was being paid the highest wages possible for a tradesman at his level. He was allowed to seek his own employment and collect his own pay, although at the end of each week he gave all his earnings to Hugh Auld. Sometimes his master would let him keep a little money, but as time passed, the hardworking young man became more and more frustrated as he gave away his money. Freedom seemed to be tantalizingly out of reach.

Still, life had improved dramatically for the former field hand. In his spare time, he met with a group of educated free blacks who had formed an educational association called the East Baltimore Mental Improvement Society. Within this group, Frederick honed his debating skills.

At one of the society's gatherings, Frederick met a free black woman named Anna Murray. A few years older than Frederick, Anna was a servant for a wealthy Baltimore family. Although a plain, uneducated woman, she was thrifty, industrious, and religious. Anna and Frederick were soon in love, and by 1838 they were engaged.

Frederick, though, was still a slave. "Give a man a bad master," he wrote later, "and he aspires to a good master; give him a good master and he aspires to be his own master." After Frederick's escape attempt, Thomas Auld had promised him that if he worked hard he would be freed when he was 25 years old. Frederick did not trust his master, and he resolved to escape. This was very difficult, however; professional slave catchers patrolled the roads on the borders between the slave and free states, and free blacks traveling by rail or steamboat had to carry official papers listing their name, age, height, skin color, and other distinguishing features.

In order to escape, Frederick had to get more money to pay for traveling expenses. Frederick arranged with Hugh Auld to hire out his time; Frederick agreed to take care of his own room and board and to pay his master a set amount each week, keeping any extra money for himself. This gave him an incentive to work harder and allowed him his first taste of living on his own.

For a few months all went well, and Frederick's savings grew. He began to study the violin and met with his friends at social gatherings held far outside the city. One day he returned late from one of these meetings and failed to pay

TO BE SOLD on board the Ship *Bance-Island*, on tuefday the 6th of *May* next, at *Afhley-Ferry*, a choice cargo of about 250 fine healthy

NEGROES,

juft arrived from the Windward & Rice Coaft. —The utmoft care has already been taken, and fhall be continued, to keep them free from the leaft danger of being infected with the SMALL-POX, no boat having been on board, and all other communication with people from *Charles-Town* prevented.

Auftin, Laurens, & Appleby.

N. B. Full one Half of the above Negroes have had the SMALL-POX in their own Country.

Slavery was growing unpopular in the North by the nineteenth century, but it thrived in the South. This newspaper advertisement announces the arrival of new slaves to be sold in the United States.

Hugh Auld on time. Auld was enraged and revoked his hiring-out privilege. Equally angry, Frederick refused to work for a week. He finally gave in to Auld's threats, but he also made a firm resolution: in three weeks, on September 3, 1838, he would be on a northbound train.

The decision was a difficult one for Frederick, and it was a mark of his character that he pursued escape so doggedly. He was going to be leaving his friends and his fairly comfortable life in Baltimore forever. He did not know when he would get to see Anna Murray again. Furthermore, if he was caught while escaping, he was sure that he would be killed or sold to slave traders. None of this weakened his resolve.

With money borrowed from Anna, Frederick bought a ticket to Philadelphia, Pennsylvania. He also had a friend's "sailor's protection," a document that certified that the person named on it was a free seaman. Dressed in a sailor's red shirt and black tie, he transformed himself from the slave Frederick Bailey to a free man of the sea.

Furtively boarding the train just as it started to move, Frederick reached northern Maryland before the conductor came to the "Negro car" to collect tickets and examine papers. This was a tense moment for Frederick because he did not fit the description on the paper he carried. With only a quick glance, the conductor walked on, and the relieved Frederick sank back in his seat. He stayed on guard throughout the rest of the trip as the train passed through the slave state of Delaware. More than once, he thought that other passengers from Baltimore had recognized him, but if so, they did not betray him.

At Wilmington, Delaware, Frederick boarded a steamboat to Philadelphia. Even after stepping on Pennsylvania's free soil, he knew he was not yet safe from roving slave catchers. He immediately inquired about directions to New York City, and that night he took another train north. On September 4, 1838, he merged with the crowds bustling "to and fro between the lofty walls of Broadway in New York."

Frederick never quite found the words to describe his feelings at leaving behind his life in slavery. "A new world had opened upon me," he wrote later. "Anguish and grief, like darkness and rain, may be depicted, but gladness and joy, like the rainbow, defy the skill of pen or pencil."

3

A Soul on Fire

Alone in New York, Frederick quickly discovered that being free did not mean being safe. From a man he met on the street, he learned that Southern slave catchers were roaming the city and hunting for fugitives in the boarding houses that accepted blacks. No one—black or white—was to be trusted.

Frederick wandered around the city for days, afraid to seek shelter or employment. Finally, he told an honest-looking black sailor about his circumstances. The man took him to David Ruggles, an officer in the New York Vigilance Committee. Ruggles and his associates were the city's link in the underground railroad, the network of people who harbored runaway slaves and helped transport them to safe areas in the northern United States and Canada.

Secure for the moment in Ruggles's home, Frederick sent for his fiancée, Anna Murray. The two were married on September 15, 1838. Ruggles told Frederick that in the port of

New Bedford, Massachusetts, a center of the American whaling industry, he would be safe from slave catchers and he could find work as a caulker. Anna and Frederick took a steamer north. Upon arriving in New Bedford, they settled in the home of the well-to-do black family of Nathan Johnson.

To go along with his new life, Frederick decided he should have a new name that would make it more difficult for slave catchers to trace him. Nathan Johnson was at the time reading *The Lady of the Lake*, a novel by the popular Scottish author Sir Walter Scott, and he suggested that Frederick name himself after a character in the book. Frederick Bailey became Frederick Douglass.

Once settled, Douglass was amazed to find that his neighbors in the North were wealthier than most slaveholders in Maryland. He had expected that Northerners would be as poor as the people in the South who could not afford slaves. Many free blacks, such as Nathan Johnson, lived better than Thomas Auld or Edward Covey. On the New Bedford wharves, he saw how industry worked when it did not depend on enslaved human muscle: in loading a ship, 5 men and an ox did what it took 20 men to do in a Southern port. Northern businesses made extensive use of laborsaving mechanical devices. To Douglass's eye, men who neither held a whip nor submitted to it worked more quietly and efficiently than those who did.

Still, New Bedford was not a paradise. Although black and white children attended the same schools, some public lecture halls were closed to blacks. Churches welcomed black worshipers but forced them to sit in separate sections, a practice that reinforced Douglass's already strong disillusionment with white clergymen. Worst of all, white shipyard employees would not allow skilled black tradesmen, such as Douglass, to work beside them.

Unable to find a job as a caulker, Douglass had to work as a common laborer. He sawed wood, shoveled coal, dug cellars, and loaded and unloaded ships. For a while, he operated a bellows in a brass foundry, where he nailed a newspaper to a nearby post so that he could read while he worked. Anna Douglass worked too as a household servant and laundress. In June 1839, she gave birth to their first child, a daughter named Rosetta. A son, Lewis, was born the following year.

ABOLITIONIST MOVEMENT

Douglass had been living in New Bedford for only a few months when a young man approached him and asked if he wanted to subscribe to the *Liberator*, the newspaper edited by the outspoken leader of the American Anti-Slavery Society, William Lloyd Garrison. Douglass immediately became caught up in the *Liberator*'s weekly attacks on Southern slaveholders. "The paper became my meat and my drink," wrote Douglass. "My soul was set all on fire."

Inevitably, Douglass became absorbed in the abolitionist movement, regularly attending lectures in New Bedford. The American Anti-Slavery Society, of which he was a member, had been formed in Philadelphia in 1833. Like Garrison, most of the leaders in the society were white, and black abolitionists sometimes had a difficult time making their voices heard within the movement. Nonetheless, the black leaders kept up a constant battle to reduce racial prejudice in the North.

Douglass also became heavily involved in the affairs of the local black community, and he served as a preacher at the black Zion Methodist Church. Among the many issues he became involved in was the battle against attempts by white Southerners to force blacks to move to Africa. Some free blacks had moved to Liberia, a settlement area established for them in West Africa in 1822. Douglass and many others in the abolitionist movement were opposed to African colonization schemes, believing that the United States was the true home of black Americans. A March

1839 issue of the *Liberator* carried some of Douglass's anti-colonization statements.

At an abolitionist meeting in New Bedford in August 1841, the 23-year-old Douglass saw his hero, William Lloyd Garrison, for the first time. A few days later, Douglass spoke before the crowd attending the annual meeting of the Massachusetts branch of the American Anti-Slavery Society. Garrison immediately recognized Douglass's potential as a speaker, and he was hired to be an agent for the society. As a traveling lecturer accompanying other abolitionist agents on tours of the Northern states, his job was to talk about his life and to sell subscriptions to the *Liberator* and another newspaper, the *Anti-Slavery Standard*. His salary was more than he could make as a laborer, but more importantly, he was doing work that he believed in with all his heart and soul.

For most of the next 10 years, Douglass was associated with the Garrisonian school of the antislavery movement. A pacifist who believed that only moral persuasion could end slavery, Garrison attempted through his writings to educate slaveholders about the evils of the system they supported. He was opposed to slave uprisings and other violent resistance, but he was firm in his belief that slavery must be immediately and totally abolished. In the first issue of the *Liberator* in 1831, he had written:

> On this subject I do not wish to think, or speak, or write with moderation. . . . Tell a man whose house is on fire to give a moderate alarm; tell him to moderately rescue his wife from the hands of a ravisher . . . but urge me not to use moderation in a cause like the present. . . . I will not retreat a single inch—AND I WILL BE HEARD.

Ever controversial, Garrison made many enemies throughout the country. Because churches refused to take a stand against slavery, he made sweeping attacks on organized religion. He also believed that the U.S. Constitution upheld slavery, for it stated that non-free individuals (slaves) should be counted as three-fifths of a person in the census figures used for determining a state's share of the national taxes and its number of seats in the House of Representatives. Because the American government was so ill founded, Garrison said, abolitionists should refuse to vote or run for political office. He also called for the Union to be dissolved, demanding that it be split between a free nation in the North and a slaveholding confederacy in the South.

Another cause that Garrison supported was political equality for women, and he fought to make it a part of the abolitionist program. Some men in the movement were opposed to him on this issue, and others thought that it distracted attention from the struggle against slavery. In 1840, when he insisted that women be allowed to serve as delegates to abolitionist conventions, much of the membership of the American Anti-Slavery Society split off and formed a separate organization. The new group, the Foreign and American Anti-Slavery Society, was not opposed to working with political organizations, and many of its members supported the small, newly formed antislavery Liberty Party.

Although the often-abrasive Garrison splintered the antislavery movement, he was a powerful leader. His sincerity and passionate devotion to the abolitionist cause impressed many men and women, and his views had a strong effect on Douglass. For three months in 1841, the ex-slave traveled with other abolitionists to lectures at meeting halls throughout Massachusetts. Introduced as "a piece of property" or "a graduate from that peculiar institution, with his diploma written on his back," he launched into stirring recollections of his years in slavery. Many of his friends in New Bedford thought the publicity was dangerous for him, but he was careful to omit details that would identify him as the fugitive slave Frederick Bailey.

SPEAKING FROM EXPERIENCE

On the lecture circuit, Douglass was an immediate success. "As a speaker, he has few equals," proclaimed the Concord, Massachusetts, *Herald of Freedom.* The newspaper praised his skill in debating, his rich voice, and his elegant use of words. "He has wit, arguments, sarcasm, pathos—all that first rate men show in their master efforts." His flashing eyes, large mass of hair, and tall figure added to his performance.

Douglass's early speeches dealt mainly with his own experiences. With dramatic effect, he told stories about the brutal beatings given by slaveowners to women, children, and elderly people. He described how he had felt the head of a young girl and found it "nearly covered with festering sores." He told about masters "breeding" their female slaves. He also used humor, making his audiences laugh out loud when he told how he broke the slave breaker Edward Covey. He especially delighted in imitating clergymen who warned slaves that they would be offending God if they disobeyed their masters.

The stories that Douglass told were just what his audiences wanted to hear. At the time, a flood of proslavery propaganda by Southern writers was being circulated to combat abolitionist literature. According to these accounts, most slaves were content with their easy life. Supposedly, slaves worked only until noon, dressed and ate better than most poor whites, and enjoyed job security that would be envied by most Northern factory workers. Many people in the North were taken in by the slaveholders' fictions, and abolitionists were often harassed by hostile mobs. Douglass's life story refuted the proslavery accounts; even so, he declared, his years in bondage would be deemed blissful by many slaves laboring in the Deep South.

After a few months of speaking, Douglass began to insert comments about the racial situation in the North. He reminded his audiences that even in Massachusetts a black man could not always find work in his chosen profession. Prejudice against

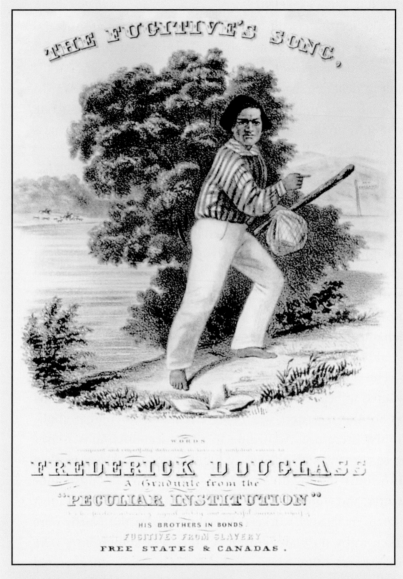

THE FUGITIVE'S SONG,

WORDS

FREDERICK DOUGLAS

A Graduate from the

"PECULIAR INSTITUTION"

HIS BROTHERS IN BONDS.

FUGITIVES FROM SLAVERY

FREE STATES & CANADAS.

Douglass traveled with his hero William Lloyd Garrison, head of the American Anti-Slavery Society, and was a star on the abolitionist lecture circuit because of his powerful stories about his years in slavery. Douglass was introduced as "a graduate from that peculiar institution" and gave credibility to abolitionists' claims regarding the horrors of slavery.

blacks was still very strong in New England. He described how he had been thrown out of railroad cars restricted to whites. Even here, he said, churches segregated their congregations and offered blacks a second place in heaven.

After Douglass's first trial period as a lecturer was over, the abolitionists asked him to continue with his work, and he eagerly agreed. During 1842, he traveled throughout Massachusetts and New York in the company of William Lloyd Garrison and other prominent speakers. He also visited Rhode Island, helping to defeat a measure that would have extended voting rights to poor whites while denying them to blacks.

Late in 1842, Douglass became involved in the case of a fugitive slave in Boston who was about to be returned to his owner. He wrote a letter to a local newspaper that helped marshal support for the runaway, and the man was eventually bought from his owner by local citizens. In 1843, Douglass participated in the Hundred Conventions project, the American Anti-Slavery Society's six-month tour of meeting halls in Indiana, Ohio, Illinois, and other states in what was then the American West.

Although Douglass enjoyed his work as an antislavery agent, his job was not all applause and glory. Traveling lecturers had to live with poor accommodations. Douglass was often roughly handled when he refused to sit in the "Negro" sections of trains and steamships. Worst of all, abolitionist meetings in western states were sometimes disrupted by proslavery mobs. In Pendleton, Indiana, Douglass's hand was broken when he and a companion were beaten up by a gang of armed thugs. Such scenes were not all that uncommon on the western frontier, where abolitionists were often viewed as dangerous fanatics. In 1837, an abolitionist publisher, the Reverend Elijah Lovejoy, had been shot dead and his newspaper office burned down by a proslavery mob in Alton, Illinois.

Despite such incidents, Douglass was sure that he had found his place in life. His abilities as a speaker grew even greater as he continued to lecture in 1844. Many abolitionists thought he was growing in ability a bit too quickly and that audiences were no longer as sympathetic to him. As early as 1841, friends had urged him to "keep a little of the plantation speech. . . . it is not best that you seem too learned." They advised that he stick to talking about his life as a slave and leave debates about the goals of the antislavery movement to men like Garrison. Some abolitionists were probably envious of his success, but others were genuinely concerned that his brilliant rise was lessening his usefulness as an agent of the antislavery movement.

To some extent, the fear proved to be correct. People gradually began to doubt that Douglass was telling the truth about himself. Reporting on a lecture that he gave in 1844, the *Liberator* wrote that many people in the audience refused to believe his stories: "How a man, only six years out of bondage, and who had never gone to school a day in his life could speak with such eloquence—with such precision of language and power of thought—they were utterly at a loss to devise." Douglass himself told of how, when walking up to the speaker's platform, he would hear people whisper, "He's never been a slave, I'll warrant you."

His reputation at stake, Douglass decided on a dangerous course. He proposed to publish the story of his life. During the winter of 1844–1845, he set down on paper all the facts—the actual names of the people and places connected with his years in slavery. When the proud author showed the finished manuscript to the abolitionist leader Wendell Phillips, his friend suggested that Douglass throw it in the fire before he was shipped back to Maryland. Douglass, however, was adamant. Even if Thomas Auld and every Southern slave catcher learned who he was, the rest of the world would hear his story too.

In May 1845, 5,000 copies of the *Narrative of the Life of Frederick Douglass, an American Slave* came off the press.

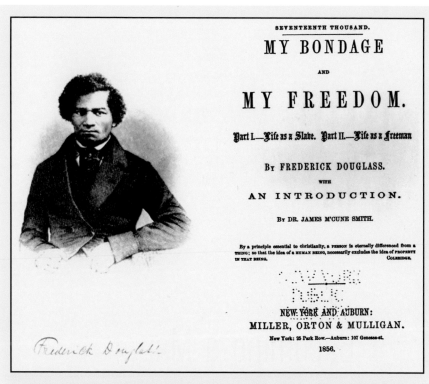

Douglass was so eloquent that some people began to doubt that he had ever been a slave. To preserve his reputation, he wrote several books, including *My Bondage and My Freedom*, and his autobiography, *Narrative of the Life of Frederick Douglass,* which became a best-seller almost immediately.

William Lloyd Garrison and Wendell Phillips wrote introductions to the book, the former ending his piece with his motto, "No compromise with slavery! No union with slaveholders!" Almost immediately, Douglass's autobiography became a best seller. Seven years after he boarded a train to freedom, he was truly in the public spotlight.

4

Becoming a Man

The tremendous success enjoyed by Douglass's *Narrative* after its publication in 1845 was due in large part to its moral force. His book is a story of the triumph of dignity, courage, and self-reliance over the evils of the brutal, degrading slave system. It is more than an autobiography; it is a sermon on how slavery corrupts the human spirit and robs both master and slave of their freedom.

The *Narrative* enjoyed widespread popularity in the North, and European editions also sold very well. Douglass's fame as an author threatened his freedom, however. Federal laws gave Thomas Auld every right to seize his property, the fugitive slave Frederick Bailey. Fear of losing his liberty prompted Douglass to pursue a dream he had long held; in the summer of 1845 he decided to go to England. There he would be safe from slave catchers, and he would have the chance to speak to English audiences and try to win support for the American antislavery movement. In 1833, the British had passed a law granting a gradual emancipation to all slaves within the British Empire, and by 1838 all were free. The vigor of the English abolition movement was still strong.

By August 1845, the Douglasses had four children: 6-year-old Rosetta, 5-year-old Lewis, 3-year-old Frederick, and 10-month-old Charles. The industrious Anna not only raised the children but also worked in a shoe factory in Lynn, Massachusetts, where the Douglasses had moved in 1842. Anna earned enough at her job to support the family while her husband was away.

Douglass sailed to England on the British steamship *Cambria*. He was forced to stay in the steerage (second class) area of the ship, but he made many friends on board and was even asked by the captain to give a lecture on slavery. Some young men in the audience were so angry about Douglass's speech that they threatened to toss him overboard. The captain told the men that he would put them in irons if they caused any trouble, and the rest of the voyage was peaceful.

For nearly two years, Douglass traveled throughout the British Isles. Everywhere he went, prominent people welcomed him to their homes. Everywhere he spoke, enthusiastic crowds came to hear the fugitive slave denounce the system under which he had grown up. He was happy in his new surroundings, free of any feeling of being a slave. As he wrote to William Lloyd Garrison in January 1846, "Instead of the bright blue sky of America, I am covered with the soft gray fog of the Emerald Isle. . . . I gaze around in vain for one who will question my equal humanity, claim me as a slave, or offer me an insult." He was astonished that he encountered so little racial prejudice among the British.

The chief topic of Douglass's lectures was, of course, slavery, but he also discussed a number of other causes that had become important to him. While in Dublin, Ireland, he spoke out in favor of the temperance movement, which was trying to

By publishing his autobiography, Douglass exposed his identity and put himself at risk of being found by his owner and returned to slavery. To protect himself, Douglass traveled to England in 1845 and spent two years touring and lecturing in the British Isles.

stop the consumption of alcoholic drinks. Douglass himself pledged to abstain from alcohol in the future. As a young man, he had hated the way slaveowners had encouraged their workers to drink themselves into a stupor during Christmas holidays. He saw alcohol as another means used by masters to humiliate their slaves. During his stay in Ireland, he also met with Daniel O'Connell, the Irish Catholic leader who was fighting to end British rule in his country. Douglass spoke out in favor of Irish independence.

In the summer of 1846, Douglass was joined by William Lloyd Garrison, and they traveled around England as a powerful team of antislavery lecturers. In Scotland, they became involved in a campaign against the Free Church of Scotland. The church was in part supported by contributions from American slaveholders of Scottish ancestry. Douglass and Garrison added their voices to the cries of local antislavery activists: "Send the money back." The church kept the money, but the dispute gained attention for Douglass's battle against American slavery.

Douglass's tour was not leisurely; during one busy month, he spoke almost every night. As usual, his blend of personal anecdotes and philosophical sermons was highly effective. For one speech, he read to the British a list of laws governing slaves in the American South: "If more than seven slaves together are found in any road without a white person, twenty lashes a piece; . . . for letting loose a boat from where it is made fast, thirty nine lashes for the first offense; and for the second shall have cut off from his head one ear; . . . for hunting with dogs in the woods, thirty lashes." He told his outraged audience that in the state of Virginia there were 71 crimes for which blacks could be executed, only 3 for whites.

In the same speech, Douglass declared, "It is necessary to resort to these cruelties in order to make a slave a slave, and to keep him a slave." He told how, when he was being beaten on Edward Covey's farm, all he had prayed for was that his life would be spared. "But," he continued, "as soon as the blow was not to be feared, then came the longing for liberty."

The World Temperance Convention that was held in London in August 1846 was the scene of Douglass's most controversial speech. There he attacked the American temperance movement because it failed to criticize slaveowners who used alcohol to pacify their work force. He also felt that the temperance activists were hostile to free blacks. The Reverend Samuel Cox, a member of the American delegation, publicly accused him of trying to destroy the unity of the temperance movement. Douglass responded that Cox was a bigot and, like many other clergymen, a secret supporter of slavery.

THE PRICE OF FREEDOM

By the fall of 1846, Douglass's thoughts were turning toward home. Garrison and other friends convinced him to stay another six months, but Douglass rejected suggestions that he settle in England. In America his people labored in bondage. There was where his work lay. Recapture remained a frightening possibility for Douglass if he returned to the United States. The problem was unexpectedly resolved when two English friends of his raised enough money to buy his freedom. The required amount, $710.96, was sent to Hugh Auld, to whom Thomas Auld had transferred the title to Douglass. On December 5, 1846, Hugh Auld signed the papers that declared the 28-year-old Douglass a free man.

Douglass appreciated the gesture of his English friends, even though as an abolitionist he did not recognize Hugh Auld's right to own him. In his farewell speech to the British people, Douglass joked, "I have as much right to sell Hugh Auld as Hugh Auld had to sell me. If any of you are disposed to make a purchase of him, just say the word." Douglass was quick to add, though, that he could not in any way condone the selling of one human being to another.

In the spring of 1847, Douglass sailed from England, once again on board the *Cambria*. He had left the United States as a respected author and lecturer; he was returning with a huge international reputation. He had left as a fugitive slave; he was returning as his own master. Thousands of people had listened

Douglass met his wife Anna, seen here, when he was still a slave living in Baltimore. Unlike Frederick, Anna was not political, which often put a strain on their relationship, but he missed Anna and his children dearly when he was away giving lectures.

to his speeches, and he had raised awareness and support for the abolitionist cause in the British Isles. His tour had been an unqualified success.

Douglass was met by happy friends and family upon his return home. Some abolitionists criticized him for letting his freedom be bought because he was thereby acknowledging

Hugh Auld's right to own him. Douglass countered that his freedom was the gift of friends and that he recognized Hugh Auld as his kidnapper, not as his master. Now that the ransom had been paid, he could fight the battle against slavery with a free mind.

During his travels in England, Douglass had demonstrated some independence from his abolitionist colleague Garrison, addressing a meeting sponsored by a rival antislavery group. Upon his return to America, he decided to found and edit a new abolitionist newspaper with the help of funds raised by his English friends. Garrison opposed this plan, saying that there were already too many such journals and that Douglass was needed as a lecturer.

Douglass dropped the idea for a while. In August 1847, he joined Garrison on a lecture tour throughout the North, and

IN HIS OWN WORDS...

The Narrative of the Life of Frederick Douglass shocked American readers with its harrowing accounts of the hardships endured by slaves. In one moving passage, Douglass detailed the uncertain future slaves faced when a master died:

Now all the property of my old master, slaves included, was in the hands of strangers—strangers who had had nothing to do with accumulating it. Not a slave was left free. All remained slaves, from the youngest to the oldest. If any one thing in my experience, more than another, served to deepen my conviction of the infernal character of slavery, and to fill me with unutterable loathing of slaveholders, it was their base ingratitude to my poor old grandmother. She had served my old master faithfully from youth to old age. She had been the source of all his wealth; she had peopled his plantation with slaves; she had become a great grandmother in his service. She had rocked him in infancy, attended him in childhood, served him through life, and at his death wiped from his icy brow the cold death-sweat, and closed his eyes forever. She was nevertheless left a slave—a slave for life—a slave in the hands of strangers.

the two abolitionists were greeted by thousands of admirers in many towns. Garrison became seriously ill, however, and Douglass was forced to continue the tour without him. After finishing the trip in the fall of 1847, he again began drawing up plans for a new abolitionist newspaper. The goal of his paper would be to publicize the abolitionist cause and fight for black equality. Rather than publish his paper in New England, where the *Liberator* was based, Douglass decided to move farther west, to Rochester, New York. Anna and the children settled into a two-story brick house that Douglass bought there, and he went to work assembling printing materials.

NORTH STAR

On December 3, 1847, Douglass began a new career when his four-page weekly newspaper, the *North Star*, came off the presses. On the masthead appeared the motto, "Right is of no sex—Truth is of no color—God is the Father of us all, and we are all Brethren." Two other black abolitionists worked with Douglass on the *North Star* for a short while. The physician and future black nationalist leader Martin Delaney was an editor, and William Nell served as publisher. Douglass's children and two young apprentices helped to set the type used to print the paper.

Once the *North Star* began to circulate, Douglass's friends in the abolitionist movement joined in praising it. Garrison and others noted the high quality of the newspaper. Not everyone was pleased to see another antislavery paper, though, especially one edited by an ex-slave. Some local citizens were unhappy that their town was the site of a black newspaper, and the *New York Herald* urged the citizens of Rochester to dump Douglass's printing press in Lake Ontario.

Gradually, Rochester came to take pride in the *North Star* and its bold editor. The town had a reputation for being strongly pro-abolitionist. Rochester's women were active in antislavery societies, and through them Douglass kept in close contact with the leaders in the fight for women's rights, among them Susan B. Anthony, Lucretia Mott, and Elizabeth Cady Stanton. Along with the good will of Rochester's abolitionists and female political activists, Douglass received encouragement from the local printers' union, whose members admired his work. (For additional information on the women's rights movement and its leaders, enter "women's suffrage" into any search engine and browse the sites listed.)

The *North Star* received a number of glowing reviews, but unfortunately the praises did not translate into financial success. The cost of producing a quality weekly was high, and subscriptions grew slowly. For a number of years, Douglass was forced to depend on his own savings and contributions from friends to keep the paper afloat. He returned to the lecture circuit to raise more money, and during the paper's first year, he was on the road for six months. In the spring of 1848, he even mortgaged his home.

In the midst of these troubles, a friend from England arrived to help Douglass with his financial problems. Julia Griffiths had raised funds to help launch the paper, and now she was prepared to fight for its survival. A good business-woman, Griffiths put the *North Star*'s finances in order, and Douglass was eventually able to regain possession of his house. By 1851, he would be able to write to his friend, the abolitionist publisher and politician Gerrit Smith, "The *North Star* sustains itself, and partly sustains my large family. It has reached a living point. Hitherto, the struggle of its life has been to live. Now it more than lives."

Despite many ups and downs, Douglass's newspaper would continue publication as a weekly until 1860 and would survive for three more years as a monthly. After 1851, it would be titled *Frederick Douglass' Paper*. For many people, Douglass's newspaper symbolized the potential for blacks to achieve whatever goals they set. It provided a forum for black writers and thinkers and highlighted the success achieved by prominent black figures in American society.

For Douglass, starting the *North Star* marked the end of his dependence on Garrison and other white abolitionists. The paper allowed him to discover in detail the problems facing blacks around the country. It also put him in contact with other black leaders, such as Henry Highland Garnet, a supporter of black emigration to Africa, and the abolitionist Charles Remond. Douglass had heated disputes with many of his fellow black activists, but these debates showed that his people were beginning to involve themselves in the center of events affecting their position in America.

Already an accomplished speaker, Douglass's work as an editor furthered his development as a writer, providing him, as he said, with "the best school possible." He honed his skills as week after week he wrote articles on important issues, an exercise that forced him to think and read and express his thoughts clearly.

By the end of the 1840s, Douglass was well on his way to becoming the most famous and respected black leader in the country. In great demand as a speaker and writer, he had proved himself to be an independent thinker and courageous spokesman for black liberty and equality. He had broken out of the bondage of his youth and had become a man.

5

The Gospel of Struggle

During his years in Rochester, Douglass continued to grow in fame as the editor of the nation's best-known black newspaper, in which he was free to attack slavery with all his power. Yet the approach of the tumultuous 1850s would severely test his faith in the ability of America to rid itself of the institution that kept his people in chains.

Some of the turmoil made its way into Douglass's home. While he had earned a reputation as perhaps the leading spokesperson for blacks, his wife, though hard working, remained uneducated and politically unambitious. Even during their years in New Bedford, friends had worried that the couple's differences would put a strain on the marriage. In 1848, hoping to bridge the gap between them, Douglass hired a teacher for Anna. The effort failed, and Anna remained almost totally illiterate.

Douglass appreciated his wife's domestic skills, but he also admired the educated, politically active women who served in the antislavery and women's rights movements. He was grateful for all the help the women abolitionists had given blacks, and in 1848, he showed his support for the feminist cause by attending the first women's rights convention. The movement drew much hostile press, and the 35 women and 32 men who went to the convention were described as "man-haters" and "hermaphrodites" (people with both male and female sexual features). The women delegates hesitated to make the demand for voting rights (suffrage) a part of their movement's platform, and the feminist leader Elizabeth Cady Stanton asked Douglass to speak on the matter. With an eloquent appeal for bold action, Douglass convinced the women that political equality was an essential step in their liberation.

The cause of women's rights would continue to remain close to Douglass's heart. Susan B. Anthony, Lucretia Mott, and many other feminists would be his lifelong friends. Perhaps it was inevitable that friendship between the handsome, articulate Douglass and one of the many women who admired him would erupt in scandal.

In 1848, Julia Griffiths began serving as Douglass's office and business manager and soon became his almost constant companion. She arranged his lectures, dealt with his paper's finances, and accompanied him to meetings. People in Rochester gradually adjusted to the sight of the black leader and the white woman strolling arm in arm down the street. Because Griffiths lived in the same house with Douglass and his wife, rumors began to fly.

Although Anna Douglass said little about the situation, she was plainly uneasy about the local talk. The controversy was even reported in the newspapers, and Douglass was attacked by the Garrisonians for involving the abolitionist movement in a scandal. In 1852, Griffiths decided to spare Douglass further embarrassment by moving out of the household. She remained his close associate until 1855, when she returned to

England. The two corresponded with each other over the next 40 years.

Tensions between Douglass and William Lloyd Garrison had been growing even before the Griffiths controversy. After Douglass moved to Rochester and started the *North Star*, he began to listen to abolitionists such as his friend Gerrit Smith, whose views on how to fight slavery differed sharply from those of Garrison. Gradually, Douglass's own beliefs began to change.

The first of Garrison's principles that Douglass began to question was the idea that resisting slavery through violent means was wrong. In 1847, he met with the militant white abolitionist John Brown, who helped to convince Douglass that pacifist means, such as moral persuasion, could not by themselves bring an end to slavery. Brown told him that slaveholders "had forfeited their right to live, and that slaves had the right to gain their liberty in any way they could." By 1849, Douglass himself was telling audiences at abolitionist meetings that he would be pleased to hear that the slaves in the South had revolted and "were spreading death and destruction." Ten years later, he had completely abandoned the idea that slavery could be ended peacefully.

As Douglass widened his circle of abolitionist friends, he also began to question Garrison's opposition to seeking antislavery reforms through the political process. In 1848, he urged women to fight for the vote. How could he deny this counsel to his own people? Garrison's view of the Constitution as a proslavery document was not accepted by all abolitionists, and as Douglass talked with these dissenters, he began to see the matter in a different light. The Constitution—with its emphasis on promoting the general welfare and securing the blessings of liberty for all—clearly seemed to be antislavery.

The North, Douglass realized, would never abolish slavery if that could only be done by dividing the Union and dismantling the Constitution. He therefore decided that slavery would have to be ended through political reforms. Through his association with Gerrit Smith, who was one of the leaders of the anti-slavery Liberty Party, Douglass began to become involved in politics. In 1848, he attended a convention of the Free Soil Party, which was battling to stop the spread of slavery into the territories west of the Mississippi River.

The final split between Douglass and Garrison occurred at the annual meeting of the American Anti-Slavery Society in June 1851. There Douglass shocked his old associates by publicly announcing that he intended to urge the *North Star's* readers to engage in politics. The Garrisonian press launched a vicious assault against him during the following months, and Douglass responded in kind. It would be many years before the breach between the two factions would heal.

The disputes between the antislavery factions did not dominate Douglass's life. He was active in any cause that furthered the progress of his people, and he attended many conventions of black abolitionists. At a meeting in 1853, he and other black leaders joined in demanding that blacks be given their full legal and political rights as American citizens. Douglass also tried to establish a black vocational school, an institution that would train its students to become skilled tradesmen. Among the people he visited in his efforts to raise funds for the school was Harriet Beecher Stowe, the author of the immensely popular antislavery novel *Uncle Tom's Cabin*. Unfortunately, Douglass was not able to collect enough money to start the school.

Although Douglass was often away from home, he was a proud and loving father. A fifth child, Annie, was born in 1849. Because Rochester's public schools refused to admit black students, Douglass at first enrolled his oldest child, Rosetta, in a private school. Even there Rosetta was segregated from white pupils, and Douglass finally hired a woman to teach his children at home. The boys also worked in the *North Star's* printing room. Never one to let racial discrimination go unchallenged, Douglass campaigned to end segregation in Rochester's school system, and in 1857 his efforts succeeded.

FUGITIVE SLAVE ACT

Events in Douglass's private life were overshadowed by Congress's struggle to decide how far slavery would be allowed to spread in the areas to the west of the Mississippi River. These territories—which would later become such states as Kansas and Nebraska—were attracting many new settlers, some of whom favored slavery and some of whom opposed it. Congress was being pressed hard to maintain a balance between the interests of the Southern slave states, which wanted no restrictions on slavery, and the Northern free states, which wanted to reserve the western territories for free labor. Congressional leaders believed that measures had to be passed to ensure that there were equal numbers of free and slave states.

In 1820, Congress had passed the Missouri Compromise, establishing a line to the north of which no slavery would be allowed in the western territories. For every slave state that joined the Union, it was agreed that one free state would also be admitted. Thirty years later, however, Northern and Southern congressmen engaged in a bitter debate over California's application to enter the Union as a free state, which threatened to upset the critical balance. The passage of the Compromise of 1850 momentarily restored the peace and conferred statehood upon California, but it also introduced the Fugitive Slave Act, which put more teeth into previous laws requiring that runaway slaves be returned to their owners.

Tensions between Free Soil advocates and proslavery supporters remained high, but the Democrat-controlled Congress continued to push for compromise. In 1854, Congress passed the Kansas–Nebraska Act, which allowed slavery to extend its reach into the northern territories in the West. The act declared that the citizens of a new state would vote on whether they wanted slavery or not. Outraged by the Democrats' appeasement of Southern slaveholders, some angry antislavery groups met to form the Republican Party.

The new party took the lead in the moral crusade against slavery. In 1857, the Supreme Court struck down almost all restrictions on slavery. In its infamous Dred Scott decision, the Court declared that slaves were property, just like a cow or a kettle; they could be taken by their masters into free states and remain legally bound to their owners. Chief Justice Roger Taney wrote that blacks "had no rights which the white man was bound to respect." The Court's shocking decision, which overturned the Missouri Compromise and the later congressional acts, gained the Republican Party thousands of new supporters and led many Northerners to actively defy the fugitive slave laws.

After the passage of the Fugitive Slave Act in 1850, Douglass became strongly involved in the Underground Railroad, the system set up by antislavery groups to bring runaways to sanctuaries in the North and in Canada. "Passengers" on the Underground Railroad often began their journey from meeting points in the hills of western Virginia and other areas close to the North–South border. From there they were moved step by step through a network of safe "stations" run by brave "conductors." The fugitives were concealed in attics and barns along the escape route until transportation could be found to the next place of refuge. They often traveled on wagons, hidden in barrels or piles of hay. Even while journeying through free states, the runaways had to be on the lookout for slave catchers and federal law officers.

The Fugitive Slave Act stated that all citizens must aid federal marshals in the capture of escaped slaves. Special commissioners were appointed to help identify fugitives, and they received a larger fee if they decided that a prisoner was a runaway.

Douglass's home in Rochester was near the Canadian border, and during the 1850s it became an important station on the Underground Railroad. Eventually, he became the superintendent of the entire system in his area. He often

After the passage of the Fugitive Slave Act in 1850, Douglass became involved in helping runaway slaves, like those shown here with Underground Railroad member Levi Coffin. Douglass's home in Rochester, near the Canadian border, became a station on the Underground Railroad, and he and his wife fed and hid hundreds of slaves.

found runaways sitting on the steps of his newspaper office when he arrived at work in the morning. At times, as many as 11 fugitives were hiding in his home. Over the years, he and Anna fed and sheltered hundreds of these exhausted men and women.

Only a few of the slaves who tried to escape from the South were successful. Douglass fiercely attacked the fugitive slave laws and the many atrocities that were being committed against runaway slaves. In a speech given in Rochester on Independence

Day in 1852, Douglass pointed out how differently blacks and whites viewed the day's celebrations:

> What to the American slave is your Fourth of July? I answer, a day that reveals to him more than all the other days of the year, the gross injustice and cruelty to which he is the constant victim . . . To him your celebration is a sham . . . a thin veil to cover up crimes which would disgrace a nation of savages. There is not a nation of the earth guilty of practices more shocking and bloody than are the people of the United States.

The sufferings of the hunted fugitive slaves reminded Douglass that freedom for his oppressed people would never come easily. In a speech he made at a Canandaigua, New York, convention celebrating the twentieth anniversary of the emancipation of slaves in the British West Indies, Douglass preached that blacks must unite to gain their liberty and that they must be prepared for a hard struggle. "If there is no struggle there is no progress," he said, characterizing those who chose to wait for freedom to be handed to them as men who "want rain without thunder and lightning, . . . the ocean without the awful roar of its many waters." Blacks, he said, would have to pay a heavy price to win their freedom. "We must do this by labor, by suffering, by sacrifice, and if needs be, by our lives and the lives of others."

JOHN BROWN

While Douglass labored with his pen and with his voice, other men chose more violent ways to fight slavery. John Brown, the white antislavery fighter whom Douglass had first met in 1847, was one of these men. Brown dreamed of setting up armed camps in the Allegheny Mountains in Maryland, Virginia, and Pennsylvania. From these bases, Brown planned to lead raids on slave plantations and to send bands of freed slaves northward. Brown had introduced Douglass to militant abolitionism in 1847, and during the 1850s he was a frequent visitor to the Douglass home, where he entertained the children by using their blocks to build models of the mountain bases he hoped to establish.

John Brown

John Brown grew up in a family strongly opposed to slavery, and this white man's antislavery views ultimately inspired him to take dramatic steps to win the freedom of an oppressed people.

Brown was born in 1800 in Torrington, Connecticut. At the age of five, Brown's deeply religious family moved to northern Ohio, to a region known for abolitionist activity. As an adult, Brown worked as a farmer, a wool merchant, a tanner, and a land speculator, traveling from Ohio to Pennsylvania, Massachusetts, and New York. He often had no money and even was forced to declare bankruptcy at one point, but his financial difficulties did not stop him from adding to his family (in addition to his 20 children, he raised a black child as his own) or from generously supporting causes in which he believed.

Brown donated land to fugitive slaves, assisted them through the Underground Railroad, and helped establish the League of Gileadites, which protected fugitive slaves from slave catchers. He eventually moved to a black community created in North Elba, New York, with a land grant from Gerrit Smith, to offer support and encouragement by setting up his own farm there.

Brown ultimately began to seek more violent means to bring an end to slavery. In 1847, he met Frederick Douglass and outlined his plan for a war to end slavery. After the meeting, Douglass noted that Brown, "though a white gentleman, is in sympathy a black man, and as deeply interested in our cause, as though his own soul had been pierced with the iron of slavery."

Brown and five of his sons fought against proslavery settlements in the territories of Kansas and Missouri. Brown also had a more ambitious plan— to arm slaves with weapons he and supporters would take from a federal arsenal at Harpers Ferry, Virginia. On October 16, 1859, Brown and 21 men (5 black, 16 white) attempted to raid the arsenal, but within 36 hours the local militia and a corps of marines led by Robert E. Lee halted the attack. Most of Brown's men were killed or captured.

Brown was wounded and captured in the attack; he then was tried and convicted of treason. He was hanged on December 2, 1859.

During the mid-1850s, Brown was the leader of one of the Free Soil bands fighting the proslavery forces in Kansas. He wanted to start a slave insurrection in the South. In 1859, he decided to lead an attack on the northern Virginia town of Harpers Ferry, seize the weapons stored in the nearby federal armory, and hold the local citizens hostage while he rounded up slaves in the area. Gathering a small force of white and black volunteers, Brown rented a farm near Harpers Ferry and made his preparations.

From the farm, Brown wrote to Douglass, asking him to come to a meeting in Chambersburg, Pennsylvania, in August. There, Brown spoke of his plans and urged Douglass to join in the attack. Douglass refused. He had agreed with Brown's earlier ideas, but he knew that an attack on federal property would enrage most Americans.

This was the last time Douglass and Brown met. On October 16, 1859, Brown and his men seized Harpers Ferry. The next night, federal troops led by Colonel Robert E. Lee marched into the town and stormed the armory where Brown's band was stationed. Brown was captured, and two of his sons were killed in the fighting. In less than two months, Brown was tried for treason, found guilty, and hanged.

Douglass was lecturing in Philadelphia when he received the news about Brown's raid, and he was warned that letters had been found that implicated him in the attack. The headlines for the newspapers' accounts of the incident featured his name prominently. Knowing that he stood little chance of a fair trial if he were captured and sent to Virginia, Douglass fled to Canada, narrowly avoiding federal officers seeking his arrest.

From his Canadian refuge, Douglass wrote letters in his own defense, justifying both his flight and his refusal to help Brown. One of the men captured during the raid said that Douglass had promised to appear at Harpers Ferry with reinforcements. Douglass denied this accusation, saying that he would never approve of attacks on federal property. Although

John Brown, seen here, wanted to end slavery with armed force, and as he planned his attack on the federal arsenal at Harpers Ferry, Virginia, he wrote to Douglass asking him to participate in the attack. Douglass refused, but letters implicated him as a collaborator with Brown, and he narrowly escaped arrest by fleeing to Canada.

he could not condone the raid, he praised Brown as a "noble old hero."

In November 1859, Douglass sailed to England to begin a lecture tour, a trip he had planned long before the incident at Harpers Ferry. As on his first visit, he was warmly received. The news of his near arrest only increased his popularity with his audiences, and his lectures helped to stir up more sympathy for the antislavery cause. In May 1860, just as he was about to continue his lecture tour in France, word reached him that his youngest child, Annie, had died. Heartbroken over the loss of the daughter whom he described as the "light and life of my house," Douglass decided to go home.

More than six months had passed since the Harpers Ferry raid, and the public furor had already died. Brown had been executed, and he was already being declared a martyr for the abolitionist cause. All charges against Douglass had been dropped. He was happy to be home.

6

The War for Emancipation

The presidential contest in 1860 featured many candidates. The Democrats had split into factions; those who were proslavery supported Vice President John Breckinridge, while moderates in the North favored the Illinois senator Stephen Douglas. Abraham Lincoln was the candidate of the Republicans, who were opposed to the spread of slavery into new territories. The candidate from the newly formed Constitutional Union Party, John Bell, was fighting to preserve national unity at any cost, and Gerrit Smith, Douglass's close friend, was running on a strong antislavery platform.

At first, Douglass campaigned for Smith, a wealthy abolitionist who had given financial support to John Brown and had backed Douglass's newspaper. A few months before the election, however, Douglass decided that Smith had no chance of winning and chose instead to back Lincoln. The Republican candidate's antislavery sentiments were well known, although he did not take as strong a position on emancipation as Douglass would have hoped.

The two Democratic candidates together received far more votes than anyone else did, but the division in the party gave the presidency to Lincoln. Unwilling to accept the results of the election, South Carolina seceded from the Union in late December 1860. Abolitionists became the targets of angry mobs in the North, which blamed them for dividing the nation. At a meeting in Boston, Douglass was thrown down a staircase.

Northern attempts to win back the South were of little use, however. In February 1861, six more Southern states—Georgia, Florida, Mississippi, Alabama, Louisiana, and Texas—seceded and established a separate government under the name of the Confederate States of America. Mississippi Senator Jefferson Davis was elected as their president.

The country waited for Lincoln to respond to the crisis. The president's inaugural address in March was a disappointment to Douglass. Lincoln promised to uphold the fugitive slave laws and not to interfere with slavery in the states where it was already established. His first priority was to restore the Union, not to end slavery.

Despairing of any hope that slavery could be ended, Douglass began to consider the possibility of organizing a black emigration to the Caribbean nation of Haiti. In 1801, a rebellion led by the great liberation fighter Toussaint L'Ouverture had defeated the French rulers on the island and resulted in the establishment of the first black republic in 1804. Believing that Haiti might serve as a good home for black Americans, Douglass made plans to sail to the island and investigate conditions there.

On April 12, 1861, Confederate troops bombarded Fort Sumter, a federal installation in the harbor of Charleston, South Carolina. The fort surrendered a day later. Lincoln called for 75,000 troops to be mustered to put down the rebellion in the South. Virginia, Tennessee, North Carolina, and Arkansas immediately joined the Confederacy. The four other slave

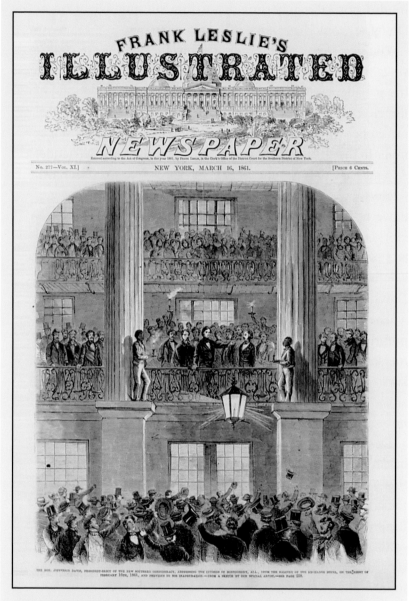

As a result of Abraham Lincoln's election as president in 1860, South Carolina seceded from the Union, followed by several other states. The states formed the Confederate States of America and elected Jefferson Davis, seen here at his inauguration, as president.

states—Delaware, Maryland, Missouri, and Kentucky—remained in the Union, although many soldiers from these so-called border states joined the Confederate army. The two sides prepared for battle, the North with its 23 states and population of 22 million against the South's 11 states and 9 million people, including 3.5 million slaves.

For Frederick Douglass and the abolitionists, the war was a battle to end slavery. Douglass's response to the surrender of Fort Sumter was one of thanksgiving. His prophecy was coming true: the nation must abolish slavery or be abolished by it. As the Civil War got under way, Douglass marked out two goals for which he would fight: emancipation for all slaves in the Confederacy and the Union border states, and the right of blacks to enlist in the armies of the North. As the war progressed, more and more people in the North would come to agree with these aims.

While battles raged throughout the South, Douglass traveled on the lecture circuit, calling for Lincoln to grant slaves their freedom. The president's actions early in the war were a blow to Douglass. When General John C. Frémont liberated all the slaves of Confederate sympathizers in Missouri, Lincoln revoked the order. He also overruled General David Hunter when the officer freed blacks captured from slaveowners in South Carolina, Georgia, and Florida. On April 16, 1862, the president signed a bill outlawing slavery in Washington, D.C., but he was slow to approve congressional measures confiscating slaves in captured areas of the South. Lincoln believed that if he passed laws that emancipated the slaves, the Union's border states might rebel and join the Confederacy.

Douglass continued to insist in his speeches and newspaper editorials that the aim of the war must be to abolish slavery and that blacks must be allowed to join in the battle for their freedom. By refusing to let blacks fight in the Union armies, the North was depriving itself of thousands of willing and able soldiers. Battlefield casualties were frighteningly high, and antidraft riots erupted in Northern cities. Blacks were frequently made the scapegoats of mobs demanding an end to the war. Meanwhile, the South's armies conscripted slaves to dig trenches and do other heavy labor. Gradually, as the costly war dragged on, with no final victory in sight for the North, Lincoln began to realize that stronger actions needed to be taken against the rebellious Confederacy.

EMANCIPATION PROCLAMATION

In the summer of 1862, Lincoln read to his cabinet a draft of an order that would emancipate slaves in the Confederate states. He decided to issue the proclamation as soon as the North won a major battle. In September, Lincoln got his victory when Northern troops pushed back a Confederate army at the bloody battle of Antietam in Maryland. On the night of December 31, 1862, the president issued the Emancipation Proclamation, declaring that as of the next day all slaves in areas not held by Union troops were free. Slavery was not abolished in the border states or in already captured areas of the South. Nevertheless, Lincoln's act freed millions of blacks, who fled from their masters and took "freedom's road" to areas controlled by Union forces.

In Boston on the night that the proclamation was announced, Douglass wrote of the spirit of those who had gathered with him at the telegraph office to witness slavery's death throes: "We were waiting and listening as for a bolt from the sky . . . we were watching . . . by the dim light of the stars for the dawn of a new day . . . we were longing for the answer to the agonizing prayers of centuries." The jubilant crowds cheered. The end of slavery was in sight.

Douglass next turned his attention to the struggle of blacks to be allowed to fight for their freedom. Early in 1863, Congress authorized black enlistment in the Union army. The Massachusetts 54th Regiment was the first black unit to be formed, and the governor of the state asked Douglass to assist

Lincoln's First Inaugural Address

President Abraham Lincoln's first inaugural address was delivered on March 4, 1861, after seven states had already seceded from the Union. Frederick Douglass was disappointed in Lincoln's speech, believing that it failed to forcefully address the issues dividing the nation. In fact, the words of Lincoln's address clearly were intended to reassure slaveholding states:

> I have no purpose, directly or indirectly, to interfere with the institution of slavery in the States where it exists. I believe I have no lawful right to do so, and I have no inclination to do so. Those who nominated and elected me did so with full knowledge that I had made this and many similar declarations and had never recanted them; and more than this, they placed in the platform for my acceptance, and as a law to themselves and to me, the clear and emphatic resolution which I now read: "Resolved, That the maintenance inviolate of the rights of the States, and especially the right of each State to order and control its own domestic institutions according to its own judgment exclusively, is essential to that balance of power on which the perfection and endurance of our political fabric depend; and we denounce the lawless invasion by armed force of the soil of any State or Territory, no matter what pretext, as among the gravest of crimes." . . .
>
> There is much controversy about the delivering up of fugitives from service or labor. The clause is now read as plainly written in the Constitution as any other of its provisions: "No person held to service or labor in one State, under the laws thereof, escaping into another, shall in consequence of any law or regulation therein be discharged from such service or labor, but shall be delivered up on claim of the party to whom such service or labor may be due." . . .
>
> I take the official oath today with no mental reservations and with no purpose to construe the Constitution or laws by any hypercritical rules; and while I do not choose now to specify particular acts of Congress as proper to be enforced, I do suggest that it will be much safer for all, both in official and private stations, to conform to and abide by all those acts which stand unrepealed than to violate any of them trusting to find impunity in having them held to be unconstitutional.

in recruitment. Douglass agreed and wrote a passionate editorial that was printed in the local newspapers. In "Men of Color, to Arms," he urged blacks to "end in a day the bondage of centuries" and to earn their equality and show their patriotism by fighting in the Union cause. His sons Lewis and Charles were among the first to enlist.

Unfortunately, Douglass's recruitment speeches promised black soldiers an equality they did not get in the Union army. They were paid one half of what white soldiers received and were given inferior weapons and inadequate training. Blacks were not allowed to become officers. Worst of all, black soldiers captured by Confederate troops were often shot.

When Douglass learned about these conditions, he halted his recruitment efforts. After publishing his complaints, he asked for an interview with the president, a request that was granted in the summer of 1863. Despite his political differences with the president, Douglass was immediately impressed by the warmth of Lincoln's personality. "I at once felt myself in

IN HIS OWN WORDS...

On March 21, 1863, Frederick Douglass published his stirring "Men of Color, to Arms!" editorial, urging blacks to join in fighting for the Union cause:

I will not argue. To do so implies hesitation and doubt, and you do not hesitate. You do not doubt. The day dawns; the morning star is bright upon the horizon! The iron gate of our prison stands half open. One gallant rush from the North will fling it wide open, while four millions of our brothers and sisters shall march out into liberty. The chance is now given you to end in a day the bondage of centuries, and to rise in one bound from social degradation to the place of common equality with all other varieties of men. . . . This is our golden opportunity. Let us accept it, and forever wipe out the dark reproaches unsparing hurled against us by our enemies. Let us win for ourselves the gratitude of our country, and the best blessings of our posterity through all time.

the presence of an honest man," Douglass wrote, "one whom I could love, honor, and trust without reserve or doubt."

Douglass explained to the president his concerns about the way black soldiers were being treated by Union officers and Confederate captors. Douglass wrote that Lincoln's response was "serious and even troubled." The president did not promise to resolve all of the problems, but he gave Douglass some encouragement that changes might be made in the future. Although not entirely satisfied with Lincoln's answer, Douglass decided to begin recruiting again.

Shortly after the meeting, Secretary of War Edwin Stanton offered Douglass a commission on the staff of General Lorenzo Thomas. Douglass accepted the offer and returned to Rochester, where he published the last issue of his newspaper. He waited at home for notice of his commission as an officer, but it never arrived.

Douglass was extremely disappointed that the commission fell through, but he continued his recruiting work. By now, Frederick, Jr., had joined his brothers in the Union lines. More than 200,000 blacks enlisted in the Union army and 38,000 were killed or wounded in Civil War battles. Comprising about 10 percent of the North's troops, the black soldiers made their numbers felt on the battlefields and distinguished themselves in many engagements. By mid-1864, the war was slowly turning in favor of the North. The South was becoming increasingly isolated as Britain and other European nations gave their support to the North.

Douglass began to focus on what the fate of blacks in America would be once they were all free. Lincoln seemed uninterested in the question of voting rights for blacks, and discrimination against black soldiers and civilians in the North continued. Douglass could not be satisfied with the liberation of the slaves alone; he wanted equality for his people. Like many other abolitionists, he did not believe that Lincoln had a strong enough commitment to improving conditions for blacks.

In May 1864, with the presidential elections approaching, Douglass attended a convention of abolitionists and zealous antislavery members of the Republican Party, who were known as radical Republicans. The delegates nominated the former Free Soil Party candidate and Union general John C. Frémont for president. The Democrats selected the popular general George McClellan to run against Lincoln on a Copperhead platform. Copperhead was the derogatory name used to refer to anyone who favored making immediate peace with the South and leaving slaves in bondage. Worried that McClellan might win the election, Douglass and other Frémont supporters decided to back Lincoln.

AN EVACUATION PLAN

Douglass and Lincoln had a second meeting in August 1864. The weary president had begun to doubt that the war could be won, and he was worried that he might have to sign a peace with the Confederacy that would leave slavery intact. Lincoln asked Douglass to draw up plans for leading slaves out of the South in the event that a Union victory seemed impossible. Douglass left the interview convinced that the humane president was a friend of blacks. He was also aware that Lincoln walked a lonely road. The president's policies were hated not only by the South but by many people in the North who had grown tired of war.

The evacuation plan that Douglass sent to Lincoln never had to be used. In the summer of 1864, General William T. Sherman and his Union troops left a path of destruction as they marched through the heart of the South. In September, Sherman entered Atlanta, the capital of Georgia, and then pressed on to Savannah, with his troops singing refrains from a popular war song, "John Brown's body lies a-moldering in the grave; His soul is marching on." The victories gave the North renewed heart and helped Lincoln win easy reelection in November. (For additional information on this and other

Midway through the Civil War, Douglass turned his attention to recruiting blacks to fight in the Union army. Unfortunately, black soldiers, like the one pictured here, were not given the equality they were promised. They were paid much less than white soldiers, given inferior training and supplies, and suffered more severe punishment when captured by Confederate troops.

battles in the Civil War, enter "Civil War battles" into any search engine and browse the sites listed.)

The dreams of the Confederacy died hard. By the end of 1864, the South was hungry and bankrupt. As the ragtag

Over 200,000 blacks enlisted in the army, making up ten percent of the North's troops and helping to turn the tide of the war. Black soldiers, like those of the 107th United States Colored Infantry, seen here, proved their equality and patriotism by fighting for the Union.

Confederate armies retreated before their better-supplied opponents, Douglass took the occasion to visit Maryland and Union-controlled areas of Virginia. He lectured in his old home town of Baltimore, where once he had toiled as a slave. Now he spoke as a free man—and an eminently successful one. On this trip, he was reunited with his sister Eliza, whom he had not seen in 30 years. He was very proud of Eliza, who through her own hard work had managed to buy the freedom of herself and her nine children.

Back in the North, Douglass attended Lincoln's second inaugural address. Standing among the crowds gathered in the nation's capital, Douglass felt himself to be "a man among men." As though to prick that bubble, government officials refused to allow Douglass or any other black to attend the evening reception in the White House. When Douglass sent word of this refusal to the president, he was quickly ushered in to the ceremony. Lincoln personally greeted him with the words, "Here comes my friend Douglass." This was indeed the man of whom Douglass would write, "In his company, I was never in any way reminded of my humble origins or of my unpopular color."

In the beginning of April, the Confederate capital of Richmond, Virginia, was captured. Lincoln himself rode through the devastated city and heard himself called "Messiah" by rejoicing blacks. A few days later, the commander of the Confederate forces, General Robert E. Lee, surrendered to the Union commander, Ulysses S. Grant, at Appomattox Court House in Virginia. On April 9, 1865, the Civil War was over.

To the horror of the newly reunited nation, President Lincoln was assassinated by a proslavery fanatic, John Wilkes Booth, while attending a play at Ford's Theater in Washington on April 14. He died the next day. With the rest of the country, Douglass mourned the man he had grown to respect.

No sadness could completely overshadow Douglass's joy at this time, however. A single, glorious fact remained: the war to end slavery had been won. All his life's work had led to this moment. Now it was here.

7

"The Work Before Us"

With the ratification of the Thirteenth Amendment to the U.S. Constitution in December 1865, slavery was officially abolished in all areas of the United States. The Reconstruction era was under way in the South, the period during which the 11 Confederate states would be gradually reintroduced to the Union. In the meantime, Northern armies continued to occupy the South and to enforce the decrees of Congress.

Frederick Douglass was 47 years old. With the war over and slavery officially abolished, he thought about buying a farm and settling down to a quiet life. Black Americans still desperately needed a champion, though, and Douglass soon rejected any notion of an early retirement.

In many parts of the South, the newly freed slaves labored under conditions similar to those existing before the war. The Union army could offer only limited protection to the ex-slaves, and Lincoln's successor, Andrew Johnson of Tennessee,

Andrew Johnson of Tennessee became president after Lincoln's assassination, but he did not share his predecessor's concern for the freedom of southern blacks. Johnson appointed proslavery governments and Southern legislatures created "black codes" that kept blacks in poverty.

clearly had no interest in ensuring the freedom of Southern blacks. The new president's appointments as governors of Southern states formed conservative, proslavery governments. The new state legislatures passed laws designed to keep blacks in poverty and in positions of servitude. Under these so-called black codes, ex-slaves who had no steady employment could be arrested and ordered to pay stiff fines. Prisoners who could not pay the sum were hired out as virtual slaves. In some areas, black children could be forced to serve as apprentices in local industries. Blacks were also prevented from buying land and were denied fair wages for their work. (For additional information on the condition of blacks after the Civil War, enter "black codes" into any search engine and browse the sites listed.)

Despite the fact that blacks were being so poorly treated in the South, some abolitionists believed that their work was done. At a meeting of the American Anti-Slavery Society in May 1865, one month after the end of the Civil War, William Lloyd Garrison had called upon the organization to disband, now that its goal was accomplished. Douglass came out against Garrison's proposal, stating that "Slavery is not abolished until the black man has the ballot." The society voted to continue the struggle for black rights, but many abolitionists left the movement.

Fortunately, abolitionists were not the only ones interested in giving blacks the right to vote. The Republican Party was worried that the Democrats would regain their power in the South. If this happened, the Republicans would lose their dominant position in Congress when the Southern states were readmitted to the Union. Led by two fierce antislavery senators, Thaddeus Stevens and Charles Sumner, a group of radical Republicans joined with abolitionists in a campaign for voting rights for black men, who, they believed, would naturally support the Republicans.

During the later part of 1865, Douglass traveled throughout the North, speaking out for black suffrage and warning the country that the former slaveholders were regaining control of the South. In February 1866, he addressed his most important audience, President Andrew Johnson. Along with his son Lewis and three other black leaders, Douglass met with Johnson to impress upon him the need for changes in the Southern state governments. The president did most of the talking, and he told the delegation that he intended to support the interests of Southern whites and to block voting rights for blacks. Douglass and Johnson parted, both saying that they would take their cases to the American people.

Despite the president's opposition, Douglass and the supporters continued to battle for black rights with some success. The public mood gradually turned against Johnson and his attempts to install governments in the South that were controlled by Confederate loyalists. The Republican-controlled Congress became increasingly resistant to Johnson's plans for a limited reconstruction of the Southern states. The radical Republicans wanted to see sweeping changes enforced that would end the former slaveholders' power in the South. Thaddeus Stevens urged that the estates of the large slaveholders be broken up and the land distributed to ex-slaves, or freedmen, as they were then known.

In the summer of 1866, Congress passed two bills over the president's veto. One, the Freedmen's Bureau Bill, extended the powers of a government agency that had been established in

Thirteenth Amendment

In December 1865, the Thirteenth Amendment to the U.S. Constitution was formally ratified. Although he initially greeted its passage with jubilation, Douglass soon realized that the abolition of all forms of slavery required more specific steps, that in order for freedom to be truly won, blacks would need economic assistance and the right to vote.

Amendment XIII

Section 1. Neither slavery nor involuntary servitude, except as a punishment for crime whereof the party shall have been duly convicted, shall exist within the United States, or any place subject to their jurisdiction.

Section 2. Congress shall have power to enforce this article by appropriate legislation.

1865 for the purpose of providing medical, educational, and financial assistance for the millions of impoverished Southern blacks. Congress also passed the Civil Rights Bill, which gave full citizenship to blacks, along with all the rights enjoyed by other Americans.

President Johnson's supporters, mainly Democrats and conservative Republicans, organized in the summer of 1866 to stop the movement for further black rights. The radical Republicans also held a meeting in Philadelphia to vote on a resolution calling for black suffrage, and Douglass attended the convention as a delegate from New York. Unfortunately, he encountered much prejudice from some Republican politicians, who were unwilling to associate with blacks on an equal level. Nonetheless, Douglass went to the convention and spoke out for black suffrage. The vote on the resolution was a close one, for some of the delegates were afraid that white voters would not support a party that allied itself too closely with blacks. Speeches by Douglass and the woman suffragist Anna E. Dickinson helped turn the tide in favor of black suffrage.

For Douglass, the convention also held a more personal note. While marching in a parade of delegates, he spotted Amanda Sears, whose mother, Lucretia Auld, had given him his first pair of pants and arranged for him to leave the Lloyd plantation. Sears and her two children had traveled to Philadelphia just to see the famed Frederick Douglass.

FOURTEENTH AMENDMENT

The movement for black suffrage grew rapidly after the Philadelphia convention. With President Johnson's supporters greatly outnumbered, in June 1866, Congress passed the Fourteenth Amendment, which was designed to ensure that rights guaranteed earlier to blacks under the Civil Rights Bill were protected by the Constitution. The amendment was finally ratified in July 1868 after all the states approved it. Although the new amendment declared that no state could deny any person his full rights as an American citizen, it did not guarantee blacks the right to vote. In most states, however, blacks were already voting.

During July 1867, Douglass was asked by President Johnson to take charge of the Freedman's Bureau, a position that would have allowed him to oversee all the government programs administering to the needs of Southern blacks. Douglass was tempted by the offer—the first major post to be offered to a black man—but he realized that by associating with the Johnson administration, he would be helping the president appear to be the black man's friend. Instead, he refused to serve under a man whose policies he detested.

By 1867, Douglass could see that Johnson's days in office were numbered. The president was unable to stop Congress's Reconstruction acts, which divided the South into five military districts and laid out strict guidelines for the readmission of the Confederate states into the Union. The new laws required the Southern states to ratify the Fourteenth Amendment and to guarantee blacks the right to vote. The radical Republicans were angered by Johnson's attempts to block the Reconstruction measures, and they instituted impeachment proceedings against him, the first time a president underwent this ordeal. The impeachment measure passed in the House but fell one vote short of the two-thirds majority in the Senate needed to remove Johnson from office. Narrowly escaping the loss of his office, the president exercised little power during the last two years of his term. (For additional information on the south after the Civil War, enter "Civil War reconstruction" into any search engine and browse the sites listed.)

During the 1868 presidential contest, Douglass campaigned for the Republican candidate, Ulysses S. Grant, the former commander in chief of the Union army. In a famous speech, "The Work Before Us," Douglass attacked the Democratic Party for ignoring black citizens and warned about the rise in the South of white supremacist organizations such as the Ku Klux

The Freedman's Bureau was developed after the Civil War to provide assistance, including education, medical care, and relief funds, to former slaves in the South. Here, freed slaves gather at an office of the Freedman's Bureau to receive rations in 1866.

Klan. These secret societies attempted to intimidate blacks with fire and the hangman's noose. They also attacked "Yankee carpetbaggers" (Northerners who had flooded into the South at the end of the Civil War) and "scalawags" (Southern whites who cooperated with the federal Reconstruction authorities).

Douglass feared that the terrorist tactics of the Klan would succeed in frightening blacks into giving up the civil rights they had gained in the South. "Rebellion has been subdued, slavery abolished, and peace proclaimed," he said, "and yet our work is not done. . . . We are face to face with the same old enemy of liberty and progress. . . . The South today is a field of blood."

Black voters came out strongly for the Republicans in the 1868 elections, helping Grant win the presidency. With Grant in office, the Fifteenth Amendment passed through Congress and was submitted to the states for ratification. This amendment guaranteed all citizens the right to vote, regardless of their race. Douglass's push for state approval of the amendment caused a breach between him and the woman suffragists, who were upset that the measure did not include voting rights for women. Old friends such as Susan B. Anthony and Elizabeth Cady Stanton accused Douglass of abandoning the cause of women's rights.

At the annual meeting of the Equal Rights Association in May 1869, Douglass tried to persuade the woman suffragists that voting rights for blacks must be won immediately, while women could afford to wait. "When women because they are women are dragged from their homes and hung upon lamp-posts, . . . then they will have the urgency to obtain the ballot," said Douglass. One of the women in the crowd cried out, "Is that not also true about black women?" "Yes, yes," Douglass replied, "but not because she is a woman but because she is black." The women in the audience were not convinced by Douglass's argument, and some of them even spoke out against black suffrage. Douglass's relationship with the woman suffragists eventually healed, but women would not receive the right to vote until 1920.

A NEW WORLD

The campaign for state ratification of the Fifteenth Amendment was successful. On March 30, 1870, President Grant declared that the amendment had been adopted. Later, at the last official meeting of the American Anti-Slavery Society, Douglass spoke gratefully about the new rights blacks had won. "I seem to be living in a new world," he said. While thanking all the men and women who had struggled for so long to make this new world possible, he modestly omitted his own name.

Still, Douglass was clearly a leader in the struggle for civil rights. By 1870, he could look proudly upon the changes he had witnessed. Between 1868 and 1870, the Southern states were readmitted to the Union, and large numbers of blacks were elected to the state legislatures. Blacks also won seats in Congress, with Hiram Revels of Mississippi becoming the first black senator and Joseph Rainey of South Carolina being the first black to enter the House of Representatives.

In 1870, Douglass was asked to serve as editor of a newspaper based in Washington, D.C., whose goal was to herald the progress of blacks throughout the country. Early on, the paper, the *New National Era*, experienced financial difficulties, and Douglass bought the enterprise. The paper folded in 1874, but for a few years it provided him with the means to publish his opinions on the developing racial situation in the United States.

Another misfortune occurred in 1872, when Douglass's Rochester home went up in flames. None of his family was hurt, but many irreplaceable volumes of his newspapers were destroyed. Although friends urged him to rebuild in Rochester, Douglass decided to move his family to the center of political activity in Washington, D.C.

During 1872, Douglass campaigned hard for the reelection of President Grant. He supported the president even though many of the Republican Party leaders he most respected, including Senator Charles Sumner, chose to back the Democratic candidate, Horace Greeley. Although personally honest, Grant was harshly criticized for not controlling the corrupt officials who served in his administration. Douglass stuck with the president, believing that blacks needed a strong friend in the White House. At the time, the Ku Klux Klan and other white terrorist organizations were burning black schools and murdering schoolteachers in an effort to keep Southern blacks from learning how to read.

Grant easily won the 1872 election, and Douglass was given an unexpected honor. He was chosen as one of the two electors-at-large from New York, the men who carried the sealed envelope with the results of the state voting to the capital. After the election, Douglass expected that he would be given a position in the Grant administration, but no post was offered, so he returned to the lecture circuit.

A third financial loss struck Douglass in 1874. That year he was offered and accepted the position of president of the Freedmen's Savings and Trust Company, a bank that had been founded to encourage blacks to invest and save their money. The previous management had made huge loans to speculators at extremely low interest rates, however. By the time Douglass was put in charge, the bank was on the verge of collapse. He immediately appealed to Congress for help and tried to restore confidence by investing much of his own money in the bank. Even so, the prestigious Freedmen's Bank failed, and many black depositors lost their money. For Douglass, it was a blow to his pride as well as to his pocketbook.

Fortunately, Douglass had the means to recoup his losses on the lecture circuit. He no longer spoke simply about black rights but included other topics on which he was an authority, such as Scandinavian folklore. On whatever subject he lectured,

DID YOU KNOW?

From the time that he first learned to read and write, Frederick Douglass determined to create a limitless future for himself, one whose boundaries would stretch to include a wide range of philosophies and areas of study. Those who met him were astonished by the broad scope of information that Douglass possessed, and by his ability to speak knowledgeably on many different topics. In 1874, after the failure of Freedmen's Bank, Douglass turned once again to the lecture circuit as a way to compensate for his financial losses. In this round of lectures, Douglass shared his expertise in a number of fields. Those who associated Douglass with the civil rights movement were often surprised to learn that he was an authority in Scandinavian folklore, a topic he had studied at length, and his lectures on the subject fascinated audiences.

he combined his humor, intelligence, and passion to create a memorable experience for his listeners. Many people described him as one of the world's greatest speakers.

As Douglass traveled, he continued the battle against the daily humiliations that blacks were forced to endure throughout the country. Whenever he encountered discriminatory practices in a restaurant, hotel, or railway car, he would write a letter of protest to the local newspapers. In 1875, he was cheered by Congress's passage of the Civil Rights Bill, which gave blacks the right to equal treatment in theaters, inns, and other public places.

In 1877, after the inauguration of the new Republican president, Rutherford B. Hayes, Douglass was finally rewarded with a political post, the largely ceremonial position of marshal for Washington, D.C. In order to court Southern votes for the close presidential election of 1876, however, the

IN HIS OWN WORDS...

On April 14, 1876, Frederick Douglass was invited to speak on the occasion of the unveiling of the Freedmen's Monument, in memory of Abraham Lincoln, in Lincoln Park, Washington, D.C. In his speech, Douglass noted that the monument was a symbol of dramatic change in American society:

Few facts could better illustrate the vast and wonderful change which has taken place in our condition as a people, than the fact of our assembling here for the purpose we have today. Harmless, beautiful, proper, and praiseworthy as this demonstration is, I cannot forget that no such demonstration would have been tolerated here twenty years ago. The spirit of slavery and barbarism, which still lingers to blight and destroy in some dark and distant parts of our country, would have made our assembling here the signal and excuse for opening upon us all the flood-gates of wrath and violence. That we are here in peace today is a compliment and a credit to American civilization, and a prophecy of still greater national enlightenment and progress in the future.

Republicans had agreed to remove the bulk of the federal troops in the South. The rights that had been granted to blacks after the Civil War could no longer be protected in the Southern states. Douglass was criticized for accepting his post after the Republicans' betrayal of their black supporters, but he saw the appointment as simply another milestone for his people. In any case, Douglass did speak out against the Republicans for abandoning Southern blacks to the terror of white mobs.

Nearing the age of 60, Douglass was ready to give up his life on the road. In his role as a U.S. marshal overseeing the criminal justice system in the nation's capital, he was aided by a large staff of employees. Following his appointment, he purchased a new home in the Washington area. The 15-acre estate that he christened Cedar Hill included a 20-room house, which held a huge library and whose walls were decorated with the portraits of Abraham Lincoln, William Lloyd Garrison, Susan B. Anthony, and other people who had influenced him. His children were frequent visitors to Cedar Hill, and he greatly enjoyed playing the role of family patriarch.

In 1877, Douglass traveled to St. Michaels, Maryland, to visit old friends and to see the farms and plantations where he had worked as a slave. While there, he took the opportunity to visit his old master, Thomas Auld. Aged and feeble, Auld greeted his former slave as Marshal Douglass, and the two men spoke for a long time. Auld both justified and apologized for his actions as a slaveholder, and the men ultimately parted on good terms.

After the 1880 election of the Republican candidate James Garfield as president, Douglass was appointed to the post of recorder of deeds for Washington, D.C. He liked his new job, which entailed managing the department that made records of property sales in the capital. During his five years in this position, he had ample time for his writing projects and speaking engagements. In 1881, he published the third of his autobiographical volumes, *Life and Times of Frederick Douglass*.

In August 1882, Anna Douglass died after a long illness. Douglass observed a traditional year of grieving, but he was hardly ready to settle into the life of a widower. He had never shrunk from controversy, and his next act upset both black and white society. In early 1884, Douglass announced that he was marrying Helen Pitts, a white woman who was nearly 20 years younger than he was.

A Legacy of Leadership

Douglass's second marriage in January 1884 aroused a storm of criticism. Many whites were outraged at him for marrying outside his race, and some congressmen called for a ban on interracial marriages in the nation's capital. Blacks felt that he was showing contempt for his race. His children never fully accepted their father's new wife, and Helen's father refused to forgive his daughter for marrying a black man.

Born of a white father and black mother, Douglass did not see anything in his second marriage that was inconsistent with his beliefs. His goal had never been a world in which black and white were separated. He believed that all people deserved justice and freedom and certain basic human rights, among which was the right to follow one's own choice in love and marriage.

A native of Rochester, Helen Pitts Douglass was an educated woman who had worked as a secretary at the recorder of deeds office. Tall and gracious, she was described by one writer as a woman who "shows the subordination of a younger person to her husband." Douglass, however, felt that in Helen he had found an equal. When asked to attend a woman's suffrage convention, he wrote back that Helen would be accompanying him for "she is not less a woman suffragist than myself." The marriage brought great happiness to both of them. A number of visitors to Cedar Hill commented on the radiance that seemed to surround the couple. "Love came to me," Helen said, "and I was not afraid to marry the man I loved because of his color."

Gradually, the controversy subsided, and Douglass was able to more fully enjoy his life. In 1884 a Democrat, Grover Cleveland, was elected president, and Douglass resigned his post as recorder of deeds shortly thereafter. As a belated honeymoon, he and his wife sailed for Europe in mid-1886. While in England, Douglass visited Julia Griffiths as well as the two women who had purchased his freedom nearly 40 years before. The Douglasses then traveled to France, Italy, Egypt, and Greece.

In 1888, Douglass made a tour of the Deep South. Seeing the shacks that poor black tenant farmers lived in, he realized that he had grown out of touch with the conditions experienced by the majority of his people. Many lived in virtual slavery. In Washington, D.C., for the 26th anniversary of the Emancipation Proclamation, Douglass spoke with rage about how blacks were being exploited and were being denied their civil rights. Five years before, when the Supreme Court had struck down the Civil Rights Act of 1875 on the grounds that discrimination practiced by individuals was legal, Douglass had bitterly protested that the Fourteenth and Fifteenth Amendments were being undermined. Now he returned to this theme.

Such speeches helped to redeem Douglass's reputation among his critics in the black community. Some people

After the death of his first wife, Douglass married Helen Pitts, seen here, a white woman nearly twenty years his junior. The marriage caused controversy in the black and white communities and even in the couple's respective families, but Douglass felt the marriage was consistent with his beliefs of equality and freedom.

thought he had grown too close to the Washington political establishment and had distanced himself from the masses of impoverished black laborers. On occasion, Douglass's ties to the Republican Party may have led him to make compromises, but he always spoke out forcefully against racial injustice.

SERVICE IN HAITI

In 1889, a Republican president, Benjamin Harrison, replaced Grover Cleveland in office. Harrison offered Douglass an appointment as the American consul-general to Haiti. His friends urged him not to take the post, saying that it was too minor for him and that the humid Haitian climate would be bad for his health. Nevertheless, he believed it an honor to serve as his country's chief representative to the world's oldest black republic, and he accepted the offer. (For additional information on the history of Haiti, enter "Haiti first black republic" into any search engine and browse the sites listed.)

Douglass and the Haitians got along very well. They were proud to be dealing with the famous champion of black rights, and he was careful to treat the small republic with the utmost respect. Unfortunately, Douglass became embroiled in the attempts of the U.S. government to establish a naval base on Haiti. He was also asked to help win concessions for American businesses. Although he believed that the United States had much to offer the impoverished Caribbean nation, he opposed the heavy-handed negotiating tactics used by his government. He knew how much the Haitians feared American domination, and they eventually did turn down the United States requests. Because Douglass refused to exert diplomatic pressure on the Haitian government, the American press blamed him for the failure to win the naval base.

By 1891, Douglass's health had begun to suffer, and he decided to resign the consulship and return to the United States. The Haitians were sorry to see him go. In 1893, as a measure of its respect for him, the Haitian government asked him to be its representative to the World's Columbian Exposition, the international fair held in Chicago. Douglass was the only black American to play an official role at the exposition, and he wrote and published a pamphlet protesting that his country was ignoring its black citizens and denying them their civil rights.

Douglass resumed his quiet life at Cedar Hill. Rising at dawn to take his stroll around the estate's grounds, he spent his mornings and afternoons writing. In the evenings he played the violin while Helen accompanied him on the piano. He also continued with his speaking engagements.

Throughout his years as a lecturer, Douglass had constantly emphasized the need for blacks to rebel against any form of racial discrimination. He also told his people that they must take advantage of educational opportunities and work hard to build a prominent place for themselves in America. To succeed, blacks had to maintain their self-respect in the face of prejudice and oppression. Douglass's speeches would strongly influence the black leaders who would follow him: Booker T. Washington, Ida Wells-Barnett, Mary Church Terrell, W.E.B. Du Bois, and many others.

In his final years, Douglass devoted much of his energies to speaking out against the country's lack of concern about the lynching of blacks in the South. Almost daily in the 1890s, new accounts were heard of black men being accused of raping a white woman and then being seized by a mob and hanged or burned to death. The crime of rape was almost never proved, but it was a charge that was sure to inflame the prejudices of white Americans and make them willing to condone the violent acts that were carried out against blacks.

Douglass made a thorough examination of the lynching issue in his essay, "The Lesson of the Hour; Why the Negro is Lynched." He placed much of the blame for the racial violence on the wealthy Southern elite, which encouraged bigoted whites to "keep the Negros in their place." Once again, he denounced the schemes proposed by leaders of both races to deport blacks from the United States and colonize them in Africa and other foreign lands. "We are here and are here to stay," proclaimed Douglass, insisting that Americans must learn to accept this fact and to make the United States a home for people of all colors.

On this note, Douglass's career came to a close. On February 20, 1895, he attended a meeting in Washington of women's rights activists. Escorted to the speaker's platform by his old friend Susan B. Anthony, Douglass acknowledged the cheers of the crowd, who applauded his long devotion to the cause of women's rights. That night, while describing the day's events to his wife, Douglass was struck by a massive heart attack and died at the age of 77.

As news of Douglass's death spread throughout the country, crowds gathered at the Washington church where he lay in state to pay their respects. Black public schools closed for the day, and parents took their children for a last look at the famed leader. His wife and children accompanied his body back to Rochester, where he was laid to rest.

A LEADER'S LEGACY

With Douglass's passing, a great era in black history came to an end. His influence went on, though, inspiring future generations to continue the struggle for civil rights.

Douglass's refusal to accept second-class status, to insist not only on greater rights but on equal rights for people of color, ensured that the Emancipation Proclamation was not an end but a beginning. His stirring speeches and autobiography shocked white Americans into recognition that slaves were not inferior beings who were somehow better off in bondage but instead were real people—people just like them.

Douglass understood that freedom and equality were not merely abstract issues, to be decided by speeches and debate, but rights that must be fought for. He recognized the value of politics in achieving these important goals and met with presidents and other politicians to convince them of the value of advancing the cause of freedom through specific, concrete

Frederick Douglass used speeches, writings, and politics to achieve rights for blacks and all minorities. His work has influenced and given hope to all those who have followed him in the struggle for civil rights.

steps. When his country split in civil war, he worked hard to ensure victory for the Union, openly urging black men to enlist and support the North. He did not abandon the struggle after America's slaves were freed but instead continued to vigilantly oversee efforts to create greater opportunities for people of color.

Douglass's stirring speeches and passionate appeals to presidents and ordinary people were echoed in the words and actions of Martin Luther King, Jr. Douglass's refusal to accept second-class accommodations or segregated transportation were a precursor to the actions of Rosa Parks and others who protested the idea of "separate-but-equal" facilities in the 20th century. Douglass even successfully fought segregated schools in Rochester in 1857, 100 years before *Brown* v. *Board of Education.*

During his lifetime, Douglass not only saw his people freed from their centuries of bondage but also helped them begin to live with whites as equal citizens in the United States. Although many of the rights and freedoms that blacks won after the Civil War were taken away from them, Douglass advised his people not to despair:

> We still live, and while there is life there is hope. The fact that we have endured wrongs and hardships, which would have destroyed any other race . . . ought to strengthen our faith in ourselves and our future. Let us then . . . resolutely struggle on in the belief that there is a better day coming, and that we by patience, industry, uprightness, and economy may hasten that better day.

1818 Born Frederick Bailey near Easton, Maryland

1824 Works for Captain Aaron Anthony

1826 Travels to Baltimore, Maryland, to work for Hugh Auld

1833 Returns to Anthony farm to work for Thomas Auld

1834 Works for Edward Covey

1835 Works for William Freeland

1836 First escape plan fails; is imprisoned; sent back to Hugh Auld

1837 Meets Anna Murray

1838 Escapes to New York; sends for and marries Anna Murray; changes name to Frederick Douglass

1841 Speaks at American Anti-Slavery Society meeting; invited to go on lecture tour

1845 *Narrative of the Life of Frederick Douglass* is published; begins tour of England

1847 Returns to the United States and begins lecture tour

1847 Begins printing the *North Star*

1848 Attends first women's rights convention

1850 Becomes involved in the Underground Railroad after the passage of the Fugitive Slave Act

1851 Breaks with William Lloyd Garrison

1859 Sails to England to begin lecture tour

1860 Returns to the United States

1863 Meets with President Abraham Lincoln to discuss the treatment of black soldiers during the Civil War

1864 Meets with Lincoln to formulate plans to lead blacks out of the South in case of a Union defeat

1866 Meets with President Andrew Johnson to discuss black suffrage

1867 Declines Johnson's offer to head Freedman's Bureau

1870 Fifteenth Amendment is adopted and blacks are granted the right to vote; becomes editor of the *New National Era*

1874 Becomes president of the Freedman's Savings and Trust Company

1877 Becomes U.S. Marshal

1880 Appointed recorder of deeds for Washington, D.C.

1882 Anna Douglass dies

1884 Marries Helen Pitts

1889 Accepts post of American consul-general to Haiti

1891 Resigns post and returns home

1895 Dies in Washington, D.C.

Douglass, Frederick. *Life and Times of Frederick Douglass.* New York: Collier Books, 1962.

———. *Narrative of the Life of Frederick Douglass: An American Slave.* Cambridge, MA: Belknap Press of Harvard University, 1960.

Foner, Philip S. *The Life and Writings of Frederick Douglass: Early Years 1817–1849.* New York: International Publishers, 1950.

———. *The Life and Writings of Frederick Douglass: Pre-Civil War Decade 1850–1860.* New York: International Publishers, 1950.

———. *The Life and Writings of Frederick Douglass: The Civil War 1861–1865.* New York: International Publishers, 1952.

———. *The Life and Writings of Frederick Douglass: Reconstruction and After.* New York: International Publishers, 1955.

Huggins, Nathan Irvin. *Slave and Citizen: The Life of Frederick Douglass.* Boston: Little, Brown, 1980.

Quarles, Benjamin. *Frederick Douglass.* Washington, D.C.: The Associated Publishers, Inc., 1948.

WEBSITES

Africans in America.
http://www.pbs.org/wgbh/aia/part4/4p1539.html

American Memory. Library of Congress.
www.memory.loc.gov/ammem/

Civil Rights Coalition for the 21st Century.
www.civilrights.org

Documenting the American South.
http://docsouth.unc.edu/douglass/menu.html

Teaching American History.org Document Library.
www.teachingamericanhistory.org/library/

Africans in America: Resource Bank
http://www.pbs.org/aia/part4/4p1539.html

ABOUT THE AUTHOR

Sharman Apt Russell received her BS from the University of California at Berkeley and her MFA from the University of Montana. She is the coauthor of *Built to Last: The Architectural History of Silver City, New Mexico*, and a feature writer for such magazines as *Darkroom Photography*, *National Gardening*, *New Mexico Magazine*, *New Mexico Wildlife*, and *Phoenix Home and Gardens*. She teaches writing at Western New Mexico University and lives with her husband and children in the Mimbres Valley of southwestern New Mexico.

CONSULTING EDITOR, REVISED EDITION

Heather Lehr Wagner is a writer and editor. She is the author of 30 books exploring social and political issues and focusing on the lives of prominent Americans and has contributed to biographies of Harriet Tubman, Sojourner Truth, Thurgood Marshall, Malcolm X, and Martin Luther King, Jr., in the BLACK AMERICANS OF ACHIEVEMENT revised editions. She earned a BA in political science from Duke University and an MA in government from the College of William and Mary. She lives with her husband and family in Pennsylvania.

CONSULTING EDITOR, FIRST EDITION

Nathan Irvin Huggins was W.E.B. Du Bois Professor of History and Director of the W.E.B. Du Bois Institute for Afro-American Research at Harvard University. He previously taught at Columbia University. Professor Huggins was the author of numerous books, including *Black Odyssey: The Afro-American Ordeal in Slavery*, *The Harlem Renaissance*, and *Slave and Citizen: The Life of Frederick Douglass*. Nathan I. Huggins died in 1989.